To

Peter

Christmas 1990

Heather

LET'S GO SKIING

LET'S GO SKIING
MARTIN BELL

PARTRIDGE PRESS

LONDON · NEW YORK · TORONTO · SYDNEY · AUCKLAND

TRANSWORLD
PUBLISHERS LTD
61-63 Uxbridge Road, London
W5 5SA

TRANSWORLD
PUBLISHERS (AUSTRALIA)
PTY LTD
15-23 Helles Avenue,
Moorebank, NSW 2170

TRANSWORLD
PUBLISHERS (NZ) LTD
Cnr Moselle and Waipareira
Aves,
Henderson, Auckland

Published 1990 by Partridge
Press
a division of Transworld
Publishers Ltd
Copyright © Martin Bell

The right of Martin Bell to be
identified as author of this
work has been asserted in
accordance with sections 77
and 78 of the Copyright
Designs and Patents Act 1988.

British Library Cataloguing
in Publication Data
Bell, Martin
   Let's go skiing.
   1. Skiing
   I. Title
   796.93

   ISBN 1–85225–111–5

Printed in Great Britain
by Butler and Tanner, Frome,
Somerset

Martin Bell

The Draumbuie Liqueur Company

CONTENTS

Ingemar Stenmark in Slalom, wearing shin pads, gauntlets and a head-guard to protect himself from the poles.

British Ski Federation

INTRODUCTION

Anyone who goes on a week's or a fortnight's ski holiday, perhaps once a year, is offered a short glimpse of another world. Their ski instructors are the immediate ambassadors of this world and its lowest citizens are the ski bums, who will do any job in a ski resort, from washing dishes upwards, just in order to get more time on the snow.

I have myself lived in this world of skiing since childhood, gradually working my way up through its ranks. If the great Downhiller Franz Klammer was known as Kaiser (Emperor) Franz, I do not know where that ranks me in the world of skiing. While *Ski Sunday*, David Vine's full-blooded commentary, and Konrad Bartelski's initial British successes did much to stimulate the profile of skiing in the minds of the British public, nothing satisfies me more than acceptance in the eyes of the people who are in the know: the coaches, trainers, and my fellow racers in the Alpine countries.

In this I am identical to the average recreational skier, who craves above all else recognition and respect from his peer group, fellow holidaymakers and class-mates in Ski School. The question is: how does he or she gain this respect? Is it through telling the right stories in the *après-ski* bar? Well, readers of this book will certainly equip themselves with the factual knowledge to do this, but I hope that this book will also equip you with the ammunition for the struggle to improve your skiing ability. Then, and only then, will you gain recognition in the only way which counts, when your friends or family stand at the bottom of the slope and say,

The Draumbuie Liqueur Company

'Oh, you've improved since last year.' For as long **Martin Bell**
as you are improving, even if that simply means
becoming more consistent or getting to know your
limits better, you can look forward to each new ski
holiday.

Even if you have to continue to spend the rest
of the year in the real world, you can depart with
confidence for one or two weeks each year to that
other world which consists entirely of breathtaking
mountains, blue sky and sparkling powder snow:
the world of skiing.

1 HOW TO GET GOING

The main reason why Swiss, Austrian and Italian children are usually better skiers than British children is that they have a natural head start: they are able to ski every weekday afternoon after school finishes at around 1 p.m. The only skiing obtainable in this country is on dry ski slopes or in Scotland. Otherwise, you need to go abroad on holiday for at least a week to make it worthwhile, although some people now go on flying visits to the Alps for long weekends.

The problem for children is that they can only take trips abroad during school holidays, unless their school organizes a school trip. Many schools already do this, and there are specialist school tour operators giving low-priced deals. If you are at a school which does not organize a skiing trip but you know that one of the teachers skis, try to persuade him to organize a trip. The school could probably run outings to a nearby dry ski slope to find out the level of interest.

DRY SKI SLOPES

As a child I was fortunate to live near the largest dry slope in Britain at Edinburgh, and through the summer I would spend one evening a week and most of the weekends training and racing there.

The first thing for the beginner to note is that the overall length of the slope is not important. What they should look for is good instruction, a friendly atmosphere, value for money and hire equipment which is in good condition. You may ask 'How can I find out this information?' The best way is to

Opposite:
Beginners can
receive instruction
at a dry ski slope.

ask other skiers, such as the staff of your local ski shop, some of whom undoubtedly will ski.

Most slopes consist of Dendix – plastic bristles similar to those on a toothbrush – and it is essential to wear long trousers and sleeves at all times, as the surface is abrasive, and gloves to protect the fingers and thumbs which can get sprained. All in all there are less injuries on plastic than on snow as the speed is lower, and some slopes are now introducing a carpet-like surface which is slower than the bristles and safer for beginners to learn on. Instruction on a dry slope will save you wasting the first few days of your precious holiday learning the basics, such as how to put your skis on, how to walk up the hill or even how to use a ski-lift, how to control your speed and direction with the snowplough, and finally, how to get up after a fall. I highly recommend that you prepare on plastic.

SKIING IN SCOTLAND

I first put skis on my feet on a trip to Cairngorm in Scotland. My parents had been interested in hillwalking and now wanted to try a holiday of a slightly different outdoor nature over the Easter break.

If you live in Scotland or Northern England, the advantage of Scottish skiing is its proximity and low cost, and you can be sure that your instruction will be of a high standard and in comprehensible English. The drawbacks are the weather and the queues. However, the weather is wet and windy rather than downright cold, and the queues, although long at weekends, are well-organized and not the free-for-all that you will sometimes encounter in the Alps. Cairngorm is sometimes closed due to high winds but the nearest town, Aviemore, has plenty of other holiday activities to offer. Glenshee, Scotland's second resort, has a ski area at least as extensive as Cairngorm's and the advantage of smaller queues, although there are not as many alternative activities. The recently opened ski area

of Aonach Mor near Fort William has the potential
to be better and larger than Cairngorm or Glenshee
when completed.

BOOKING A HOLIDAY ABROAD

Tour operators are now training travel agents to
know enough about the ski holidays they are selling
to find the right kind of holiday for each client, but
it still pays to learn how to read a brochure and pick
out the vital information.

SNOW

One essential ingredient of a ski holiday is snow
and the part of the brochure which will tell you
the most about that commodity is the *piste* **map**
which is supplied for each resort. The altitude of
the village and of the highest point of the lift system
should be marked, usually in metres. Obviously, the
higher you go, the greater the likelihood of snow,
and above 3,000 metres (approximately 10,000 feet)
you are likely to be skiing on a glacier, or more
accurately on snow which is retained there all
year round by the cooling effect of the mass of
ice beneath it. Summer skiing on glaciers is quite
enjoyable, although you have to be up early to
take advantage of the snow while it is still firm
from the overnight frost. The lifts close around
noon when the snow becomes too slushy, leaving
your afternoons free for activities such as tennis,
swimming, mountain biking or sunbathing. Quite
apart from summer skiing, a resort with a glacier
will guarantee you some skiing even during the
mildest of winters.

Piste maps also show where there are trees, which
is important during bad weather and **white-outs**,
when diffuse light makes it impossible to tell the
snow and sky apart. Runs through trees add some
contrast and it is easier to orientate yourself than
out in the open. The **tree-line** is usually at around
2,000 metres in the Alps, although if you are skiing
at more southerly latitudes, such as the Pyrenees or
Colorado, the tree-line will be higher, and you will

have to go higher to be sure of finding snow.

The *piste* map will also tell you the standard of difficulty of the runs, ranging from the easiest green runs to the most difficult black runs. If you are a beginner, look for green runs (**nursery slopes**) near the village, rather than ones which can only be reached via a cable-car which you will have to queue for in the mornings and travel back down on in the evenings.

RESORTS

There are three types of ski resort. First-generation resorts are the large towns which were already in existence before skiing came to the Alps, such as Kitzbühel or St Moritz. Second-generation resorts, such as Val d'Isère or St Anton, were mere hamlets in the early part of this century, and have grown simultaneously with the growth of skiing as a tourist industry. Third-generation (or purpose-built) resorts, such as Les Arcs or Tignes, were built in uninhabited, high altitude areas during the last few decades, specifically to enable people to walk out of their front door and go skiing with the minimum of fuss.

Kitzbühel: the Downhill course is fenced off, and finishes right in the village.

Courtesy of the Austrian National Tourist Office

LIFTS

First-generation resorts are generally situated low in a valley, so that it is necessary to take an access lift, usually a **cable-car**, up to areas where there is snow. Plenty of ski-lifts will fan out from the top of the access lift, but skiers travelling up in the mornings and down in the late afternoon (if there is insufficient snow to ski down to the town) will create a bottle-neck and sometimes queues up to an hour long will form.

Purpose-built resorts have lift systems designed to eliminate bottle-necks, and, on the whole, the planners have learnt from the mistakes of the first-generation resorts. These resorts will only suffer from large queues during busy times of the season.

The lift systems of second-generation resorts obviously fall somewhere between the two extremes. Their lifts were probably built in a haphazard way, but, because they are usually situated higher up than first-generation resorts, there are more ski-lifts fanning out from the village itself, and you are more likely to be able to ski down to the village at the end of the day.

Of course it is impossible to generalize and many first-generation resorts are now building new access lifts to take the pressure off the old cable-cars. Much depends on the type of lift built and its capacity (the number of people it can transport up in one hour). For example, some of the older lifts have capacities of four or five hundred, whereas modern ones have capacities of over 1,500. Cable-cars, although they usually take forty or fifty skiers (sometimes over 100) at a time, have low capacities because there are only two cars on the wire and they have to stop each time to load people on. **Gondolas** (also known as *télécabines* or bubbles) carry two–six people, usually seated, in small enclosed cars spaced roughly 50 metres apart on a wire which is constantly moving. It is a very civilized way to travel, especially in bad weather and is much better than being crammed into a cable-car with forty-nine people with BO and

OFVW Markowitsco

St Anton, and its funicular lift. alcoholic breath first thing in the morning. Six-man gondolas have very high capacities. **Chairlifts** have an advantage over gondolas in that you do not have to remove your skis every time, although a long, slow chairlift ride can be a cold experience. **Detachable quads** are chairlifts which, like a gondola, detach from the wire at the top and the bottom to allow people to get on and off, as the wire itself moves at very high speed. These chairlifts carry four at a time and therefore have very high capacities; they are common in North American resorts, where they are known as line-munchers, line being the American word for queue.

On the nursery slopes you will often start on

a **babylift**, where you simply hang on to a wire at waist-height. They often have bars attached to the wire which you can hook round your behind to take the weight off your arms. Then you will graduate on to a **T-bar**, where two skiers are pulled up the hill by a T-shaped bar attached to an overhead wire. The most common mistake made by beginners on this type of lift is to try to sit down on it; it will not support your weight and you have to stand upright and allow yourself to be dragged up by it. It is therefore also known as a **draglift**. Make sure you ride the T-bar with someone of roughly your height and weight, otherwise it becomes unbalanced and difficult to ride. That problem is eliminated with the **button-lift** or **poma**, where you are dragged up on your own by a round plate hooked between your legs. Pomas are usually faster, but less sociable than T-bars, where chance encounters are often made.

If you fall off a draglift of any kind, it is vital to let go of the bar at once to avoid **If you fall off a draglift let** being dragged up on your stomach. **go of the bar at once** If you can, get off the track and out of the way of other skiers as quickly as possible.

A **funicular** is a cable railway where two trains balance each other and go up and down alternately. It has a fast journey time and good capacity.

The prices of **lift passes** vary from resort to resort, and are usually listed separately in the brochure, in local currency. The actual cost to you will depend on the exchange rate at the time.

ACCOMMODATION

Accommodation varies from country to country. French purpose-built resorts offer plenty of self-catering apartments which are good value but usually quite cramped. As a rule of thumb, if an apartment is advertised to sleep four, it will be comfortable for two people to eat, sleep and live in. The availability of these apartments is often in one-week packages only, from Sunday to Sunday, but they are still good value even if you are not staying that long. The main expense is obviously food, and as the *supermarchés* in the high-level resorts have a captive market, they are fairly expensive. It is better to bring supplies out from Britain or to stock up in a *hypermarché* down in the valley on your way. This is only an option if you are driving out in your own car.

All ski resorts have hotels. In Austria there is a large range from pensions, which sometimes only offer bed and breakfast, to establishments which are really quite luxurious, with large rooms, saunas, jacuzzis and indoor heated pools. There are many new buildings, but they always make sure that the traditional architectural style is maintained. In contrast, hotels in French ski resorts are not as luxurious but are still fairly pricey. This has prompted British tour operators to offer chalet holidays, where they employ cheap seasonal staff (cooks, waitresses, maids) from Britain, known as chalet-girls, in buildings which they have rented for the season. These can vary from genuine six-person chalets where one chalet-girl will do all the cooking, serving and cleaning, to buildings which were previously locally run hotels, sleeping as many as eighty guests and employing up to twenty staff.

One thing to bear in mind for all types of accommodation, especially in the larger resorts, is their distance from the nearest ski-lifts. The brochures are never too precise on this point and rarely provide a street map (rather than a *piste* map) of the resort, but you can usually get one from the tourist office of the country involved. (*See* Chapter 7 for addresses.)

TRAVEL

The four main types of travel to a ski holiday are: air, coach, train or self-drive. Of these, the first two are the most popular.

On a **charter flight package tour**, as a rule, you will not experience delays at the departure airport, as the traffic is not as heavy as in summer. The

problems usually occur when trying to land at a continental airport in winter weather: if there is fog, the aircraft will have to divert to another airport, adding a couple of hours on to the transfer time to the resort. Most charter flights are on Saturdays, which means with more people travelling on the weekend, the coaches will be delayed in leaving from a busy Munich or Geneva airport as passengers and baggage are assembled. In addition, the roads themselves will be busier and so the overall transfer time on a Saturday will probably be longer than listed in the brochure. Some operators now use Sunday flights as a selling point.

The most to be said for **coach** trips is that they are cheaper than flying and slightly less fatiguing than driving yourself. The constant video films which are necessary to alleviate the boredom of those who cannot sleep are a nuisance to those who could possibly have done so. There is an advantage, however, if you have large amounts of luggage, as all your bags and skis are loaded aboard the coach when you leave and you do not have to worry about them until you reach your hotel. The same applies

Avoriaz: a futuristic resort but with traditional transport (no cars are permitted in the resort).

to the homeward leg of the journey, if you wish to bring back your full duty-free allowance, which is also an advantage of the self-drive holidays. As the coach leaves the resort on the evening of the transfer day (usually Saturday) rather than in the morning you have one more day at the resort than if you travel by plane.

Train travel to the Alps is obviously the transport of the future. Once the Channel Tunnel is finished we are promised a journey time of four hours from London to Paris and there are already *Trains de Grande Vitesse* taking less than four hours from Paris to Bourg St Maurice, the nearest station to resorts like Val d'Isère or Les Arcs. Changing stations in Paris will always be a headache however and at present the best connection is the Arlberg Express, which can take you direct from Calais to Zürich, St Anton and Innsbruck. The French *couchettes*, or six-person sleeping compartments, are fairly comfortable and safe, and it is a very atmospheric way to travel, rattling through the night. Of course, resorts like Wengen, Mürren, Saas Fee and Zermatt are only accessible by train, so you might as well go the whole way by rail. They are all situated in Switzerland, where the connections are frequent and so punctual that you can set the proverbial watch by them.

The **self-drive** option can be worth considering if there are the right number of people in the car: ideally three. If all three can share the driving, then you will have to drive only one third of the time **Self-drive *can* make your** and can sleep the rest. It means that **holiday easier and cheaper** the ferry ticket across the channel, which in any case is far cheaper in winter than in summer, works out cheaper per person than with one or two travellers. Finally it means that the car is less cramped than with four or more travellers, so it is still possible to stretch out and get some sleep. It is often said that the time of year when you take your holiday influences the decision whether or not to drive, as there is more daylight and probably less snow on the road in March or April than in December or January. That is true but you should always expect snow in the mountains, so ideally you should fit snow-tread tyres and certainly carry snow-chains as a back-up. Studded tyres are not suited to the long *autoroute* (or *autobahn*) haul before you get to the Alps. Obviously you need to make sure of overseas motor insurance. The main advantage of self-drive is flexibility once you are in the Alps, if you want to try out some other ski areas, or if you are going to a large town like Innsbruck.

It is perhaps apparent that I am speaking from experience here, and in fact I have made more journeys to the Alps than I am able to remember; certainly over 100. I was eight when I started travelling to Switzerland by train without my parents, although in a supervised group of kids with my ski club. One time I missed the train on which the club group was travelling, so my father took me as far as Ostend on the far side of the Channel, and deposited me on a direct train to a Swiss station where I would be met. As I was only nine years old at the time, this was a big adventure and journeying to Europe by rail is still the mode of transport which holds the most romance for me. Later, when I was at school in Austria for four years, I usually travelled by train and can remember vividly my trip out to start the first term: the sun rose as we were passing Lake Zürich, and Switzerland was looking picture-postcard perfect. In all those years of travelling by overnight train, I never had anything stolen, nor was I threatened in any way.

When I was first on the British Ski Team we used to drive out to the Alps and back in a slow minibus, sometimes taking thirty hours from Edinburgh to the Alps. I learnt how to drink endless cups of coffee to stay awake at the wheel (others just chewed dry coffee beans); the most demanding time of all was the graveyard shift from 3 a.m. to 5 a.m. When my brother, Graham, and I moved to Harrogate we were given a sponsored car by the owner of the dry ski slope there, which speeded up our journey time. By staying overnight with a fellow ski-team member in Surrey, we were able to catch a 6 a.m. ferry from Dover and make it out to the Alps by that evening, cutting out the overnight drives and the graveyard shift! After another couple of years the British Ski Federation achieved enough sponsorship income to be able to fly us out to the Alps, whenever possible using the chartered flights of tour operators who gave us good deals. It changed the quality of our training dramatically, as we no longer had to spend the first two days of our precious time on snow simply recovering from the fatigue of the journey, and we were able to leave our equipment and vehicle with our Austrian trainer.

The mode of transport of which I have had the least experience is the coach trip: indeed I have only made two, which was quite enough!

One thing I have never had the experience of is fatherhood, but the commonly held view is that families taking a ski holiday are best advised to travel by air, as the sheer duration of the other methods of travel make it impossible to keep the children occupied. Self-drive holidays give some flexibility to families travelling with small children, as you can choose when to stop for those necessary breaks.

WHEN AND WHERE TO GO?

Obviously, families are often limited to travelling in the school holidays, but if you do have a choice then the time of year you take your holiday is very important. In December you should only consider **The time of year you take your** high altitude resorts, if possible with **holiday is very important** a glacier, to be sure of having enough snow, as the large dumps of snow have been coming particularly late in recent seasons. Over the Christmas and New Year period you will also have to contend with long queues for the lifts, except for early in the morning on New Year's Day!

Austrian hoteliers refer to the *Jännerloch*, or January hole, and it is true that demand for rooms (and therefore hotel prices) drops in the middle two weeks of January when the holiday period is over. So if you are prepared to put up with the chance of very cold conditions and slightly meagre snow conditions, you will get a cheaper holiday with shorter queues in the middle of January. However, the most desirable time to go skiing is not until February, when the sunshine becomes a little stronger but the snow cover is still at its maximum.

After the ideal conditions (and high-season prices and queues) of February, the stronger sunshine begins to take its toll on the snow cover, and in late March and April you would once again be advised to stick to high-altitude resorts. The compass indicator on the *piste* maps can give you added insight into the mountain on which you will be skiing. North-facing slopes will be in near-permanent shade and bitterly cold in December and January, whereas south-facing slopes are preferable at this time of year. In March and April, however, the south-facing slopes will be the first to turn brown as the sun burns off the snow.

The type of resort is more important than the country

The type of resort (e.g. first-generation or purpose-built) is more important than the country in which it is located, but of course skiing in each country has its own atmosphere.

Austria has plenty of traditional villages with quaint wooden barns and onion-steepled churches. Most resorts are second-generation at low altitudes, with much of the skiing on runs cut through pine forests. The larger resorts have done much to upgrade their lifts recently. The food is somewhat dull, but the night-life is very lively, as the Austrians are a friendly people who are equally happy organizing modern night-clubs and traditional wood-choppers' folk dances; anything to make money from their northern neighbours, the West Germans, who are by far the most numerous tourists in Austria.

The **Swiss** are a more restrained and orderly

nation than the Austrians, but many of their resorts have a great tradition of welcoming British visitors, who actually helped to invent the sport of ski-racing in resorts like Mürren and Wengen in the 1920s. The villages are, if anything, even more quaint than in Austria, and the whole country is impeccably clean and well-kept, as befits one of the richest nations (per head of population) in the world.

Italy is generally scruffier, but with the largest share, by area, of the Alps, there is a wide range of types of resort. The food is excellent (if you like pasta) and the overall life-style is very relaxed.

The **French**, like the Italians, are less ready to speak English than the Austrians and Swiss, but most resorts are very aware that the British are the largest source of income outside of French holidaymakers and are doing their best to welcome them. The planners are now regretting the purpose-built concrete apartment blocks of the past and are now insisting on traditional stone for new buildings in many resorts, but traditional Alpine charm is still not one of France's strong points.

As well as skiing in the Alps, it is also poss-ible to book holidays to other areas such as the Pyrenees (Spain, France and Andorra), Eastern Europe (Yugoslavia, Bulgaria), Scandinavia and North America.

You can get very reasonably-priced holidays to **Bulgaria** due to its weak currency and to **Andorra** because it is a tax-free zone. The advantage of **Scandinavia** is its miles of uninhabited pine for-ests, perfect for getting away from it all on a pair of cross-country skis, but like Eastern Europe and the Pyrenees the mountains are not as high as the Alps and the runs are shorter and less varied.

Recently the **USA** and **Canada** have become popular destinations with British holidaymakers. There are slight differences in the skiing between the two countries, but a greater distinction has to be made between the nature of the ski resorts in the East and the West of the continent.

The hills in the East are generally of a fairly low

altitude and the runs are shorter than those found in the Alps. The main centres of population are in this area, however, and so there are large numbers of resorts which cater for weekend and daily skiers. The Eastern climate is bitterly cold and with relatively little snowfall, so the use of snow-making cannons has become commonplace. These devices spray water under pressure from nozzles spread out at regular intervals along the main runs, which are connected to an underground piped water supply. Many large Alpine resorts have now installed snow-making machines, but the technique was pioneered in the Eastern USA, where conditions are ideal for the process: low temperatures and low humidity. (The fact that Britain's winters are exactly the opposite – warm and wet – means that it will always be very difficult to apply snow-making in this country, although some systems operate in temperatures as warm as freezing-point.)

Unfortunately snow-making often produces icy conditions, so when skiers want to find powder snow, they head for the Rockies, in the West. The high altitude, low humidity and the relatively large distance from the sea, produce light, dry snow which can be skied in fairly easily even at waist-depth. The runs are as long as those, at most Alpine resorts, and there is plenty of space on the well-groomed *pistes* for high-speed cruising. There is a macho attitude towards skiing difficult mogul runs, and a few steep slopes are always left ungroomed. But if you should chance upon one of these double diamond runs by mistake, there is always an alternative, easier way down.

All North American ski areas are extremely well-regulated and safety-conscious. There is a perimeter fence around the skiable area, beyond which you are not allowed to cross without a guide, the ski patrol will caution people who are skiing out of control, and the queueing when necessary is fair and civilized. There are no problems with draglifts as almost all the lifts are chairlifts, which can sometimes lead to a long, cold ride.

The accommodation in North America is always of a luxurious standard and the service is extremely hospitable. Canadians are particularly pleased to greet someone from the old country and in the USA they are very friendly when they hear a British accent.

The only drawbacks are the lack of character of the resorts, most of which look the same, and the exaggerated sincerity of waiters, ski-lift attendants, etc., can become slightly overbearing after a while.

So the best thing to do when booking a ski holiday is to choose the type of resort which best suits your requirements, not necessarily confining yourself to any particular country. Then choose the type of accommodation, the mode of travel to the resort, **Choose the type of resort,** and the time of year when you would **accommodation, travel and time of** like to take your holiday, although **year, *then* choose a tour operator** in some of these areas you may be restricted by work, school or family commitments. Only then should you look for the tour operator which can fulfil all these requirements for the lowest possible price.

LEARNING TO SKI

Skiing is not a sport which you can teach yourself. You could conceivably learn from watching other skiers which positions you have to adopt, but you would not know the correct moves which have to be made to get your body into those positions. You need to be taught the easiest types of turn first, and then when you can apply that turn, to manoeuvre yourself around the ski area (sticking to the easier runs) with confidence. Later you can move on to more difficult types of turn which allow you to ski faster, more elegantly, and more efficiently. Through all these stages you will need an instructor, who can tell you what moves to make, whether you are making the wrong moves, and what it will feel like when you hit upon the right moves.

Whether you are on a dry ski slope in Britain,

or on snow in Scotland or abroad, there are two means of access to a **ski instructor**: through Ski School, where classes of roughly ten skiers are assigned to an instructor according to their ability; and private lessons, when you hire an instructor for a one-to-one session (or possibly accompanied by one or two other people).

Ski School is acknowledged as the best way for beginners to have fun while learning to ski. As long as the class is not too big, the instructor is able to give everyone the very simple hints that will teach them to stop and turn using the snowplough, and anyone who is having problems will be reassured by the fact that everyone else is making just as big a fool of themselves, rolling around on the snow or Dendix.

Private lessons are more useful if you feel that you have reached a plateau in your development and wish to make the breakthrough into a more advanced way of skiing. The instructor will be able to spend his whole time watching you and is far more likely to pick up any minor errors which you may be making and which would not be noticed in a Ski School class. The one-to-one situation can also be useful if you are lacking in confidence and feel that you will always be bottom of the class in Ski School, although if the instructor is not very understanding, a private lesson can sometimes be detrimental, because he will make everything look effortless and simply show up your own attempts.

When you book a holiday, remember that Ski School will not be included in the price of the package, and make sure that you find out how much it will cost before you choose a resort. But also enquire as to what service you will receive for that price. For example, the *Ecole du Ski Français* is very expensive, but you have the right to priority on the lift queues when you are with a class.

Once you are enlisted in the Ski School, make sure that you get value for money. If your instructor's English is not good enough then you should demand a replacement, and it is worth registering a complaint if the size of your class gets up to around the twenty mark. Do not feel inhibited about going to the boss of the Ski School with your complaints. If you can show him that you are the kind of person **Do complain if you are not getting the** who will kick up a stink and poss-**standard of service you expect** ibly deprive him of trade from British tourists in future, he is more likely to intervene and do something about your problems. This will apply especially in Austria, where the monopoly of one Ski School per resort has only recently been repealed and no-one will want to look bad next to the competition.

Traditionally, Austrian and Swiss Ski Schools have the better reputation of English-speaking instructors, whereas French and Italian ones can be problematic. But it is impossible to generalize: one valley in the Italian South Tyrol is populated by inhabitants who are tri-lingual, speaking German, Italian, and Ladinisch (a local language deriving from Latin), and to them English is just one more tongue which presents little difficulty. And of course if you go on holiday to a resort which is popular with the British, such as Val d'Isère or Les Arcs, almost all the Frenchmen will speak good English.

Someone who will undoubtedly speak perfect English, but who is no substitute for an instructor, is the **ski guide** provided free of charge by most reputable tour operators. His job is to show guests who do not know the resort which runs are the most enjoyable, which part of the mountain has the best snow conditions at present, and which lifts are the best to take to avoid queues and bottle-necks.

Generally the ski guides are fairly competent (although if it is their first season in the resort they will obviously know it better in April than in December) but what they are not allowed to do is teach. There has been quite a lot of local resentment towards them, especially in Austria (because of the recent monopoly) and in France, which is the only Alpine country which does not accept foreign instructors' own domestic qualifications and requires that they take an exam (called the *equivalence*) which checks that their ability is up to French standards. The French may not be able to continue this restrictive practice in the post-1992 free market. Some resorts have even gone so far as to stipulate that the ski guides are only allowed to operate on the first couple of days of each week, to introduce the guests to the resort.

Another group who have reason to resent the ski guides (partly because of the misleading similarity in the names) are the **mountain guides**, who are the only people qualified to take clients skiing off-*piste* (i.e. on parts of the mountain which have not been prepared and made safe by the lift company). This requires special expertise (which we will deal with in Chapter 3) and you should never venture off-*piste* with only a ski instructor or ski guide.

All in all, most resorts accept that the ski guides are an extra service offered by the tour operator which will entice clients to their village and bring in revenue.

HOW TO GET INTO SKI-RACING

I entered my first-ever race when I was eight. It was on a dry ski slope course which was barely 6 seconds long, and I surprised myself by winning. The first prize was a reduced-price trip to Switzerland for Junior race-training with a British Alpine club. There are several such clubs in Britain, based in no one particular part of the country, each club having a resort in the Alps where it has long-established links with the locals. Some of the clubs date back to, and in fact helped to organize, the beginnings of ski-racing as a sport in the 1920s.

When my parents had picked me up from Victoria Station after that first-ever race-training trip abroad and were driving me home, I cried in the back seat of the car because I would not see any of my new-found skiing friends until the following Christmas, when the next race-training was due to be held. At the end of that second trip, the club

Martin Bell preparing to compete in the British Junior Championship, aged nine.

decided to enter me, at the age of nine, for the **British Junior Championships** where the upper age limit was sixteen, and my ski-racing career had begun.

One year later I suffered my first setback: a broken leg. I missed the season's races but was able to get back on skis again at the very end of the season, during the Easter holidays. My club was not running a Junior race-training that Easter but they arranged for me to stay at their usual resort with Toni, a regular trainer for the club. That Easter, he was training the local Swiss village kids, so I was allowed to join in and soon made up for the time which I had missed.

Since I took up racing, the training of Britain's Junior skiers, between the ages of fourteen and eighteen, has been taken over by the **English Ski**

Council and the **Scottish National Ski Council,** who use the British Junior Championships to spot talented youngsters from the various British Alpine racing clubs. As well as this route of entry into the Scottish and English Junior Teams, the English Ski Council selects racers who have come directly from race-training organized by local English ski clubs (each based at its own particular dry ski slope), on the basis of their success in races held on the plastic. Similarly, the Scottish National Ski Council selects Juniors directly from local Scottish clubs such as the Lothian Ski Racing Association or the Aberdeen Ski Club, most of whom run race-training at their local dry ski slope and at the Scottish ski area which is nearest to them. There is a full circuit of races on snow for Juniors in Scotland, held at different ski areas, but unfortunately, international competitions are few and far between in Scotland, so British youngsters cannot match themselves against the world's best skiers of their own age (or learn by imitating them), purely by racing in Scotland.

Scotland also has races on the plastic, notably at Hillend Dry Ski Slope near Edinburgh, the longest and steepest slope in Britain. In England this is the only form of ski-racing possible, with three levels of races on the circuit: **Qualifying races, Mid races,** and the **Grand Prix** series. If you are considering training with a club at a plastic slope, find out from the English Ski Council when the next race is taking place in your area, and go along and watch. You can find out which of the clubs in your area has good coaches and a keen attitude towards race-training, by looking at the performances of their racers. Remember that the size of the slope is not always important and that some small slopes have a long tradition of racing.

The results of all these races (plastic races in England and Scotland, races on snow in Scotland, the British Junior Championships and other races held in the Alps by the English Ski Council and the British Alpine racing clubs) are compared by means of a system of **British Seed Points**. The winner of a race is awarded a number of points (the race penalty) depending on the existing points of the racers whom he has beaten (i.e. the standard of competition of the race). The lower the penalty, the better the race. Every other racer who finishes the race is awarded the race penalty plus extra points calculated from his time deficit to the winner. At the end of the season, each racer's two best (i.e. lowest) points results (three best on plastic) are averaged to give him his points for the following season. In races on snow, the racers with the fifteen best points are sent down the course first (in random order), followed by the rest, in order of points ranking. This is because the course becomes more rutted and difficult to ski as the race goes on, so it is a vital part of ski-racing to improve your points as soon as possible, in order to get the best conditions. On plastic, the conditions do not vary and the best racers are sent down last to ensure a dramatic climax.

The best racers from the ages of seventeen to twenty-one are selected for the **British Development Squad**, which is run by the **British Ski Federation**.

The Development Squad is chosen primarily from racers on the English and Scottish Junior Teams, but selection is possible for racers who have only trained with British Alpine racing clubs or with local clubs on the continent. This is to provide a route into the British Team for talented British youngsters who live abroad and who are therefore not part of the English or Scottish scene and have not been noticed by the English or Scottish Junior Teams.

Racers on the English and Scottish Junior Teams are encouraged to start racing in international races run by FIS (*Fédération Internationale de Ski*) as soon as possible. Results from all over the world, from World Cups and Olympic and World Championships down to the standard FIS race are compared by means of FIS points, along the same lines as the

British Seed Points system. An added refinement is that the world ranking of each racer is worked out and shown on the list. As there are over 5,000 racers on the FIS points list this is no mean achievement and is made easier by the use of computers. There are separate lists for the four disciplines: **Slalom**, **Giant Slalom**, **Super Giant Slalom**, and **Downhill**.

The British Development Squad, comprising the C Team and the D Team, is selected on the basis of FIS points, and it is from the best of these racers that the **British Ski Team**, comprising the A Team and the B Team, is chosen, on the basis of world rankings. The British Ski Team has no upper age limit.

All the racers on the British Team and the Development Squad must be full-time and have finished their education, but for younger racers there is the problem of combining large amounts of skiing with a full-time education.

Between the ages of fourteen and eighteen I attended a school of skiing excellence in Austria, for which I had to take an entrance examination consisting of a ski-race, basic physical coordination tests, and a written test, in German, on grammar and simple mathematics. I was proud to be accepted into the school, and was lucky to be joined by another British boy who had already spent four years at another Austrian school and who was able to help me with the language problems. The fees were not high, as ski-racing schools are heavily subsidized by the Austrian government. There are similar schools in France, Sweden and the USA (where the cost is higher but there is no language problem), and an English-speaking school in Villars, Switzerland, which does not concentrate on competitive skiing to the same extent. Recently, a British Ski High School has been set up in France, with British teachers and curriculum, and no doubt it is there, and in Scotland, that sufficient numbers of ten- to fourteen-year-olds will be trained, to produce a strong future British Ski Team.

2 EQUIPMENT

MINIMUM CLOTHING REQUIREMENTS

Skiing is a sport that requires a fairly large amount of expensive equipment. However, most of the major items can be hired, so it is not worth buying any more than you really need, at least until you know whether or not you like skiing.

Most of the articles of clothing which you will need to buy for your first ski holiday will come in handy on cold winter days back home. Items such as gloves, a warm hat, sunglasses and a weatherproof jacket need not spend fifty weeks of the year (between ski holidays) inside the wardrobe. In fact, the only two special pieces of equipment that you need to buy for skiing are **overtrousers** and **goggles**.

When learning to ski, you will inevitably fall over a few times. This will usually be quite a comfortable experience, as the snow is soft, but unfortunately it is also wet. Your hands will often be the first part of your body to touch the snow and for this reason your **gloves** have to be waterproof. Woollen gloves are not good enough; leather is the best material, **It is *never* advisable to** although you can get very good **do without gloves** waterproof gloves made from manmade fabrics which are slightly less expensive than leather. Whatever you get, you can make your gloves last many more years by treating them regularly with waterproofing silicone spray. It is better for your gloves to be slightly loose-fitting than too tight, as tight gloves restrict the circulation in the fingers. Loose-fitting gloves also mean that you can pull your fingers down out of the fingers of the gloves and bunch them into a fist to warm them up, at times when you are not actually using your hands. (For example, when riding up on a chairlift.) Of course, mittens achieve the same warming effect all the time, but they make fiddly operations more difficult. (For example, unzipping the top of your jacket to show your lift pass, which is usually worn round the neck on a piece of string.) It is never advisable to do without gloves, even if it is a warm April day and you feel sure that you will not have any falls. The large-granuled snow which is common in spring is very abrasive to the skin. (Skiing in a bikini or shorts is not a good idea, for the same reason.) Your hands can get wet for reasons other than a fall; when you pick up your skis at the end of the day, to carry them back to your hotel, they are bound to be wet and covered in snow.

A **hat** is necessary on cold days, as body heat can be lost very rapidly via the scalp. If it is snowing, an extra problem is wet hair, which is a perfect ingredient for a holiday-wrecking cold. Hats come in all shapes and fabrics, so choose whatever you look best in, but remember that you will only get maximum use from it, if it is something that you can wear down the High Street at home. The only point to make sure of is that the hat comes far down enough to cover the ears, as these are often the first extremities to feel the cold. In dry, medium cold weather, a headband is often enough to keep the ears warm.

Baseball-style peaked caps may be trendy, but as soon as you get up some speed the wind catches under the peak and flips the cap off your head, leading to an annoying walk back up the hill to fetch it. Really cool skiers wear their baseball-caps back-to-front to avoid this. In fact the Japanese Slalom racer, Okabe, has been known to race in a back-to-front cap!

The types of **sunglasses** used for skiing do not really differ too much from those used for driving or for sunbathing. However, they are even more necessary for eye protection, because of the amount of harmful rays reflected off the snow. In fact, the snow reflects almost all the light which shines on it, so your skin and eyes have to contend with double the usual amount of sun rays; almost as much from below as from above. As with many pieces of ski equipment, paying a higher price will guarantee you better quality, and there are several well-established brands of sunglasses whose main selling point is their special lenses which cut out harmful rays. If you have particularly sensitive eyes, and are going skiing in the spring, or in the summer on a glacier (where there are more harmful rays due to the high altitude), it is advisable to use mountaineering glasses, which have leather shields on each side to stop light getting in from behind. Anyone who skis without eye protection is risking snow-blindness, a painful condition which often does not manifest itself until the evening, back down in the valley.

There are now so many different styles of ski-wear available that you will have to make your own choice of 'look'. However, there are certain aspects of design which are necessary for comfort and effectiveness. The first choice is whether to buy a one-piece ski suit or separate jacket and overtrousers. A **one-piece** outfit will usually look very stylish, but it is inconvenient for several reasons. Obviously, the biggest nuisance occurs when there is an abrupt rise in temperature, either on a hot sunny day in spring, or due to entering a warm, muggy bar at 5 p.m. for some *après-ski*: unless the suit has a zip around the waist, it will be impossible to remove the upper half and you will have to tie it around your waist, making you look suddenly a lot less stylish. For beginners, a one-piece suit is not a good investment, as they do not know whether they will become regular skiers and they want a jacket that they can use back in Britain as well. For racers who want to get down into the aerodynamic crouch, known as the tuck, fairly often, one-piece suits can sometimes be

Tony Stone Worldwide/Mark Junak

One-piece suits can be useful when powder skiing; they stop the snow getting up your back.

constricting along the length of the back, unless they are exactly the right cut for that particular person.

When buying a **ski jacket**, it is always useful to have a good look at the label, and not only for the price! If you want a particularly waterproof jacket, check the label to see if its outer shell is made of a water-resistant fibre such as Tactel. For additional protection, it may have an inner waterproof but breathable membrane such as Gore-Tex. This will allow your perspiration to escape out of the jacket, and avoid any damp build-up of sweat, which could give you a chill later on when the temperature drops. Obviously, if you are skiing non-stop mogul runs in 20°C, even Gore-Tex will not stop you from getting very sweaty! A good indicator of a warm jacket, which you will need if the temperature is −20°C, is the filling. Down has now been superseded by man-made fillings, and if the label tells you that the jacket contains a reputable brand of filling, such as Neidhart, you can be sure it will be warm. As a general rule of thumb, if the label does not sing the praises of the materials used in the jacket, they are probably not of the highest quality and the price should be correspondingly lower. Incidentally, the label 'Made in Hong Kong' does not indicate low quality, as there is considerable ski-wear manufacturing expertise in the Far East, due to Japan's large ski market.

A good jacket should be elasticated around the waist, and not ride up too high when you raise your arms, or else the kidneys can catch a chill. The cuffs on the arms should have inner, elasticated cuffs, fairly high up the wrist, as well as an outer cuff which will fit over the glove and ideally have velcro to tighten it up. You need plenty of pockets, inside and outside, to carry sunglasses, suncream, money, etc. The zips should all be plastic, as metal ones can freeze up in low temperatures. The main zip should have an outer flap over it, fastened with poppers or velcro, to keep the wind out. The collar should be high and wide enough to fit around your lower face (up to the nose), and there should be an inner flap of material to stop the zip rubbing against your mouth, which can be unpleasant in cold temperatures. A hood, concealed inside the collar behind a zip, is not essential, but can be useful to stop your woollen hat getting soaked if you ever have to suffer the miserable experience of skiing in the rain.

The only garment which you need to buy specifically for skiing and which will seldom be put to use back in Britain (except when sledging, hillwalking in rain or sleet, or just messing about in the snow), are waterproof **overtrousers**. The most suitable type for beginners are salopettes, which have a warm filling like a ski jacket, and a high waist with braces to stop snow getting down the back of them when you have your inevitable falls in the snow. When buying a pair, check for similar signs of quality manufacture as with the jacket. You should have no problem matching the trousers with the jacket in terms of colour and style. One thing to make sure of is that the bottoms of the legs of the salopettes are loose enough to fit over a pair of ski boots. Do not worry, you will not be re-introducing flares! Check on the fit, if necessary using a pair of boots, in the shop where you are buying the salopettes. Inside the main leg cuff, there should be a thin, waterproof elasticated cuff which will stretch tightly over the boot and stop snow going down your boot or up your leg.

It is best to wear long thermal underwear, a pair of tights or tracksuit bottoms under your salopettes. On warm days you may not need them, but take them along on your holiday and experiment, remembering it is always better to be too warm than too cold.

It used to be fashionable to wear stretch ski pants made from a Lycra-type material, but these are never very warm and are best seen in good weather or in 1960s Bond films! They are, however, used by Slalom racers, who wear ski pants with heavily padded knees and shins to protect them from the Slalom poles which they hit. Another version of trousers worn by racers are overtrousers with zips along the entire length of each leg, to enable them to be taken off without removing their boots or skis. Generally this is done moments before the start of a Giant Slalom or Downhill, as the racing outfit is an aerodynamic suit which provides little protection against the cold.

The other item of equipment which you will have little use for when you return home (unless you are a motorcyclist), are **goggles**. But on a ski holiday, they are essential, for snowstorms (where the snow would blow in through the sides of your sunglasses) and for cold days (where even the slight rush of wind at low speeds will cause most people's eyes to water). The optical qualities of the goggles are just as important as for sunglasses, as you will sometimes end up wearing them on sunny days when your eyes will need protection from harmful rays. The other things to check for are that the goggle frame fits comfortably on your face, that you have enough peripheral vision, and that the strap fits fairly tightly around your head (also with your hat on).

Skiers always wear their goggle strap over their hat, for the simple reasons that it helps keep the hat on and that it makes it easier to remove the goggles (e.g. to clean them) without removing the hat. On the forehead, it is best to place the upper edge of the goggles on top of the lower edge of the hat, overlapping by about a centimetre. Otherwise, a gap would appear between goggles and hat and you could get a very cold forehead. In Canadian ski resorts, where the temperatures are sometimes very low, this is known as the gorby gap, gorby being a Canadian derogatory term for a beginner.

Most goggles are available with different colours of lenses: dark ones for sunshine, yellow or orange ones to improve the visibility on foggy days. You are best advised to buy one of each colour and discover which ones you prefer by trial and error. I know some racers who wear nothing but dark lenses and others who wear only orange ones. An important thing to check for, however, is that you are able to change the lenses very easily, as you may have to do this with cold, uncooperative fingers (e.g. if you scratch a lens and want to replace it), and some manufacturers' models are easier than others.

The final purchase which you will need to make, unless you have some left over from your summer holiday, is suncream. The same rules apply as for your eye protection; remember that your face will be exposed to more powerful rays than on a summer beach, partly because of the altitude and partly because of the rays reflected back up off the snow. Lip protection is very important, as the wind and low humidity can dry them out, and if you have sensitive lips it is worth investing in some white zinc cream, which totally blocks Ultra-Violet rays. For summer skiing on a glacier this is a necessity, otherwise you may come home with painful open sores on your lips.

SKIS, STICKS, BOOTS AND BINDINGS

If you are a beginner who knows nothing about ski equipment, you will almost certainly hire the hardware (skis, sticks, boots and bindings) for your first ski holiday. The staff of the ski shops are usually knowledgeable and helpful, but if you already know the characteristics and terminology of the equipment, you will have a better chance of asking for exactly what you want. Should you have to make any complaints, it will make more of an impression on the shop assistant if you know (at least partly) what you are talking about.

As with a ship, the front end of a ski is the sharp end. It is known as the **tip**, and is not only tapered to a point but is curved upwards to help the ski ride over lumps and bumps in the snow. Incidentally, the tips on Downhill racing skis are much flatter, as Downhill courses are well-prepared and the ski does not have to contend with bumps and moguls; a smaller tip means less weight at the front of the ski and less vibration at high speed. The back end of a ski is the **tail**. The underside of the ski (the part which runs on the snow) is the **base**, bordered on either side by the metal **edges**, which are necessary to help the ski grip when turning, and divided down the middle by the **groove**, which is supposed to keep the ski going straight when it is not turning. Some recent models do not have a groove.

Looking along the ski you will notice that it is wide at the tip, narrower at the middle (in the area where your foot will be), and wide again at the tail. This characteristic is the **sidecut** of the ski and is the main factor in making the ski turn; the more exaggerated the sidecut, the shorter and more sudden the turns the ski will make – it will be more responsive.

When you place the ski on a flat surface, you

will see that the middle part is raised above the tip and tail; this is the **camber** of the ski. It makes the ski springy and accounts for the acceleration achieved by racers at the end of each turn. After a certain amount of use, the ski eventually loses its camber and becomes dead.

Bindings are devices which are permanently screwed on to the ski and into which all ski boots can be fastened, thereby attaching the ski to your leg. When you hire your first pair of skis you may not even realize that the binding is an entirely separate piece of equipment; it will soon become clear, however, when you buy your first skis and need bindings to go with them, that there is a large choice of brands, each with their own advantages of safety, convenience and price.

Safety is the most important function of modern ski bindings. In the days when the foot was fixed permanently to the ski, the ski was like a giant lever, increasing the twisting forces on the leg whenever the skier fell. Now they are designed to release the boot from the ski as soon as the twisting forces reach the danger level (i.e. whenever the skier falls). Occasionally a skier may hit a bump or hole with such a jarring effect that the binding will release although the skier has not fallen. The binding 'thinks' that the skier is about to fall and this is known as a pre-release. Safety bindings have dramatically reduced the number of skiers coming home with broken legs over the last ten or twenty years.

Ski boots have two small ridges, one on the toe, one on the heel, which clip into the **toepiece** and **heelpiece** of the binding. Most modern bindings are step-in, which means that you do not have to bend down to do them up; simply line up your foot and stamp down with your heel. All bindings are required by FIS rules to have a **ski-stopper**. This device, also known as a **ski-brake**, has two prongs which drag in the snow whenever there is no boot in the binding. This means that a ski which has come off in a fall does not slide off down the slope, gather

momentum, and impale someone.

The simplest items of hardware are the **ski sticks**. In America they are known as ski poles, and if you ever ski in Australia you will hear them referred to by the German word *stocks*. They are used by beginners to stop themselves from setting off down the hill until they are ready to do so. Advanced skiers

Front-entry (*left*) and rear-entry (*right*) boots. Ski design and graphics are becoming ever more adventurous.

plant one stick in the snow before each turn, to aid balance and rhythm. All skiers use them to push themselves across a flat piece of hillside.

The handle at the top of the stick has a strap, which stops you from dropping the stick should you momentarily lose grip of it. The correct way to hold the stick is to put your hand upwards through the strap and then grip downwards on to the handle and strap together, but the strap should not be too tight, so that if the stick catches in a rope or fence you can let go of it without it taking your hand with it.

The lower end of the stick has a sharp point to help it sink into ice, and about 10 centimetres above the end a round plastic plate, roughly 10 centimetres in diameter and known as the **basket**, is attached to the stick to prevent it from sinking too deeply into soft snow.

Your **ski boots** can have more effect on the enjoyment of your holiday than any other piece of equipment; if they are uncomfortable, life on **Uncomfortable ski boots will make life** the slopes can become a misery.
on the slopes miserable Modern boots are constructed from stiff plastic which prevents any lateral movement of the ankle. If you wish to edge your ski, simply tilt your knee inwards and the action will be transferred directly to the ski. The efficiency with which a boot does this is known as edge control. In addition to this outer plastic shell, there is an inner boot or liner made from soft foam which will adapt itself to the shape of your foot. With some models the inner boot can be removed to make drying easier.

There are two different designs of shell with different methods of unfastening to allow the skier's foot into the boot. Front-entry boots are the traditional design; they open up at the front and fasten up by means of four clips or buckles which snap tight across the front of the foot and ankle. Advanced ski technique requires that the skier can flex the ankle forwards against the front of the boot, but there must be some stiff resistance from the boot against the shin, to prevent the ankle from reaching its limit of mobility. Front-entry boots have the advantage of allowing the skier to vary that resistance according to taste, by varying the tightness of the front clips.

Rear-entry boots have a section which folds down at the back to allow the foot to enter and which then fastens by means of a clip round the back of the ankle. There are internal straps which hold down the ankle and front of the foot to prevent them from moving around, but in general these can be left on a certain setting and all you need to deal with when putting on and removing the boots is the one clip at the back. So they are certainly more convenient, and they have the reputation of being more comfortable than front-entry boots, although this is often a matter for personal preference.

SKI AND BOOT HIRE

Many skiers put skis on their feet for the first time at a dry ski slope, almost all of which have ski- and boot-hire departments. Usually, the staff will ask beginners for their standard shoe size and hand them ski boots of the same size to try on. Most beginners make the mistake of waiting until they are out on the slope until they discover that the boots are uncomfortable. It is worth staying in the ski-hire department for a few minutes, to test the boots for comfort. It is not enough to walk up and down in the boots; you should also test them in the positions you will get into while skiing, by leaning forward and pressing your shins against the fronts of the boots (good technique), and by leaning backwards against the high backs of the boots, a bad position but one you are bound to get into occasionally. If your boots are too short for you it will soon become evident in this position as your toes will be pushed against the end of the boot. You should simulate the snowplough position by standing on the two inside edges of the boots. If the boots are uncomfortable, it may be because they are the wrong size, which can be easily remedied, or it may be because you have certain pressure points which occur with all boots because of the shape of your feet. If this is the case, all you can do with hired boots is use larger boots and put foam around the pressure point, cutting a hole in the foam where the actual area of pain is, to take the pressure off it and distribute it equally on to the surrounding area. Where do you get the foam from? Well, it is certainly worth asking at the dry ski slope itself, but if they have none then you can buy some from a hardware shop and bring it along on your next trip to the slope.

Once you have been issued with your boots at the ski hire, someone will size you up and give you a pair of skis which are roughly the same length as your height. You will then need to give both skis and boots to one of the ski-hire staff to have the bindings adjusted to your boot size, standard of skiing and weight. Binding manufacturers produce models which will adjust to a very large range of sizes, specifically for ski-hire use, and this will take very little time. One model known as the Integral system has gone one better and produced boots with two ridges on the sole which are a standard distance apart (no matter what size the boot) and fit into special bindings which never need to be adjusted for size.

The tension of the springs in bindings decides how much force is needed to cause them to release during a fall, and this can be adjusted on all bindings. If you gave a pair of bindings which had been adjusted for a child to a 15-stone adult, he would probably pop out of them merely by leaning forward. Similarly, an advanced skier will exert a fair amount of force through the binding in the course of a routine run down a mogul-field and will not want it to pop off, whereas beginners are going very slowly (and exerting small forces on their bindings) when they fall over, but their skis should still come off. So the bindings must be adjusted for weight and skiing standard, and you must honestly divulge both these statistics to the expert who is fitting your bindings.

Most dry ski slopes simply have several cartons of ski sticks of differing lengths which they will allow customers to choose themselves. First, they will tell beginners that your sticks should come up to your elbow when you are standing straight with your arms straight down by your sides. The sticks at dry ski slopes will have no straps as the point of the stick can sometimes get stuck in the matting or in the earth underneath, which would jar your arm if your hand were in the strap. Baskets are obviously not necessary as deep powder snow conditions are rare in Britain! Some dry slopes dispense with ski sticks entirely for beginners, reasoning that they have enough unfamiliar pieces of equipment to contend with in any case and will not need sticks until learning more advanced turns.

On a ski holiday abroad, the skis and boots are generally available for hire in the resort once you arrive, which is the most sensible option. It is possible to hire skis in Britain (at ski shops and even at Gatwick Airport) before departure, but you then have to cart them out to your destination along with the rest of your baggage. Airlines, however, do not apply excess baggage charges to skis and it can be worth taking equipment with you if you are going to a remote ski area which may not have a ski-hire shop. (No package tour destinations come into this category.) If your feet are a peculiar shape and are uncomfortable in most models of ski boot, it may be worth hunting around for a suitable pair before you go, as there is no guarantee of finding a comfortable pair at your destination.

Once in the ski-hire shop in the resort, many of the rules are the same as those for the dry slope ski hire. It will probably be your first morning, the sun may be shining and you will be itching to get out into the winter wonderland, but a few extra minutes trying different boots until you are sure that you have found a comfortable pair will save hours of pain later on.

A better condition of ski is to be expected than on dry ski slopes, where the higher friction of the

Dendix wears holes in the base and blunts the edges in a fairly short space of time. In fact, you should look out in particular for holes in the base which are so deep as to reveal the metal layer below, and edges which are completely round. (This can be tested by dragging the thumb or fingers over the edge in several places along the ski.) Racers' edges are sometimes so sharp that you could literally shave with them, but recreational skis must merely feel fairly sharp to the touch. You have a right to ask for another pair of skis if the ones they give you do not match up to these criteria, but if they do not comply there is little you can do, other than take your business elsewhere, if indeed there is another ski-hire shop in the village. Most shops are very conscientious and spend many hours repairing skis before the start of the season. The problems occur when there is a shortage of snow and skiers are hitting rocks more frequently than the shops can cope with.

If you are in doubt as to how sharp your edges should be, or how big a hole in the base has to be before it becomes unacceptable, the tour operator's representative or ski guide will be able to advise you. Your ski instructor could also give you useful advice, but remember that it is not unknown in some villages for the same person to be the boss of the Ski School and the owner of the local ski shop!

BUYING YOUR OWN EQUIPMENT

For reasons which have already been made clear, the first and most important piece of equipment worth investing in is the ski boots. Someone whose skiing is not yet of a high standard will find it hard to tell the difference between different types of ski other than differences in their length or their state of repair. But it is all too easy to tell the difference between comfortable and painful boots. Not only will owning your own boots guarantee that you will always be comfortable and happy in them, but in addition if any pressure points or sore spots should develop, you can alter them in ways which would not bring smiles to the faces of ski-hire staff if you used such methods on their boots. The easiest way to remove a pressure point (if the inserting of extra foam with a hole does not work) is to cut away some of the outer surface of the inner boot, assuming you can remove the inner boot to gain access to the part you want to work on. It is also possible to grind away some of the inner surface of the outer boot, or to push out and stretch an area of the outer boot (after having softened it with a hot air blower). These techniques require special tools which you may be able to get hold of from the British importer of the boot, whose address you should get from the retailer who sold you the boots.

Remember when buying your boots that a racers' model of boot will not help you if you are not of that standard and in fact it will probably hinder you by making you ski permanently in an awkward and exhausting position with your knees bent at right-angles!

When buying skis, the same rule applies. Buy the model which is designed for your standard of skiing. For example, beginners' skis are designed to skid (as in snowplough turns) in a **Buy equipment suited to your** stable and constant manner. But rac- **standard of skiing** ing skis are designed to carve turns and even if you are trying to do skidded turns on them they will have the tendency to try to run along the edge, which will cause them to go straight on, unless you have applied enough pressure to achieve reverse camber of the ski and carve the turn. If you have not heard any of this terminology it means that you are not yet ready to buy racing skis!

The best people to tell you what standard of ski and boot would suit you are instructors who have seen you ski, either abroad or at home on the dry slope. It is sometimes better value to buy skis abroad, but remember that you will have to pay customs duty on goods purchased in non-EEC countries like Austria.

Buying equipment for children is obviously a problem, as they outgrow skis, boots and ski-wear almost every year. Enquire at your local ski slope and if you are lucky, there will be an annual second-hand ski equipment sale in the area, usually held in the autumn. Boots are the only items of equipment that are sometimes not suited to second-hand use, as a new boot moulds itself to the shape of its first owner's foot and will not usually change after that. But if a second-hand boot is definitely comfortable, it is usually a good bargain. Second-hand skis are also bargains, but if you buy them with the bindings already fitted, beware of binding models which are not stiff enough or too stiff for your weight or standard of skiing: both will be dangerous.

In general when buying bindings it is best to rely on knowledgeable staff at ski slopes. All binding manufacturers now train their dealers and you have a right to ask whoever is selling you your bindings whether he has been on one of these training courses. Although binding manufacturers are always coming up with new selling points (the latest being bindings which allow the ski to flex more fully, something only of use to skiers of racing standard), there is in reality far less difference between different manufacturers' models than between a well-adjusted and wrongly-adjusted binding of the same model.

Mounting of the bindings on to the skis is not difficult provided you have the right tools: basically, a drill bit of the right length so that the holes do not go right through the ski, and a template (known as a jig) which shows where the holes have to be drilled. After that the bindings can be screwed in, with a little glue in the holes beforehand. Most ski shops can do all this, but you need to take your boot along to the shop as normal bindings (as opposed to ski-hire models) cannot be moved backwards or forwards very far once they have been mounted and therefore have to be mounted in roughly the right place. The toe of the boot should be exactly in the middle of the ski as the ski is designed to perform at its best with that particular weight distribution.

So, when buying second-hand skis with bindings already fitted, check that they are roughly in the right place for your boot size (otherwise they will have to be re-drilled), that they have roughly the right strength of spring for your weight and ability (all bindings are calibrated on the same scale, known as DIN), and once you have bought them take them to a ski shop to have the exact adjustments made.

SKI PREPARATION

David Vine, on *Ski Sunday*, is always at great pains to stress the importance of the **waxing** and its influence on the racers' performances. It is true

Graham Bell sharpening the edges of a Downhill ski with a fine file. Recreational skiers should hold the file at right-angles to the base.

that we spend many hours waxing our skis and that a bad wax job could cost a racer as many as 4 or 5 seconds over a 2 minute Downhill (enough to send him from 1st to 50th), but the absolute basic ingredient, without which a racer would simply skid off the course in a race like the Hahnenkamm in Kitzbühel, are properly prepared edges. Beginners, intermediates, and even racers will notice far more easily whether their edges are sharp or blunt (if they are skiing on icy or hard snow) than whether their skis have been waxed correctly or even at all.

Furthermore, it is the texture of a pair of Downhill skis which determines whether they will be fast or slow, and although it is possible to spoil a fast pair by waxing them wrongly, it is impossible to improve a slow pair with any amount of waxing. In general, rough bases run better on warm, wet snow, while smoother bases are required for colder snow (below $-10°C$).

SPECIALIST EQUIPMENT FOR RACING

If you are a young, up-and-coming racer, the first discipline which you will compete in is Slalom. It requires a smaller slope (and indeed can be done on dry slopes), necessitates less physical strength, and produces less speed (and is consequently safer) than any of the other Alpine disciplines. It is therefore an excellent introduction for young racers. Later in life, usually in their late teens, they will have to decide whether to specialize in Giant Slalom, Super Giant Slalom, or Downhill, or to remain Slalom specialists for the rest of their careers, depending on what discipline they are physically or mentally best suited to. A precious talented few will succeed in becoming all-rounders, achieving world-beating performances in all four disciplines: a slightly larger minority will excel in three out of four disciplines.

But when you are first introduced to Slalom, the immediate priority will be to protect yourself against the **slalom poles**. In any race it is important to take the shortest possible route from the start to the finish, and in ski-racing this means getting your skis as close as possible to the gates around which you have to turn. But centrifugal force dictates that even in a technically perfect racing turn your body will have a slight inside lean, and if your feet are already as close to the slalom pole as it is possible to get, much of your body will be on the other side of the pole, and a certain part of your body will hit the pole and knock it flat. Fortunately modern slalom poles fall flat quite easily, thanks to a spring-loaded hinge situated at the point where the pole protrudes from the snow. This has the added benefit of making the pole pop back up once a racer has passed, ready for the next racer.

It is a common fault among young racers to forget that they have to get close to the pole with their feet and they tend to lean in and reach with their hand to punch the pole. Once they improve, the pole is often still hit with the hand, but it is more of a fending off action to protect another part of the body which the pole would otherwise hit, rather than a reaching action to try to hit a pole which they would otherwise miss completely. In any case, the hands are the first part of the anatomy needing protection, and it is possible to buy **gauntlets** which have padding almost up to the elbow, or forearm pads which fit from the wrist to the elbow. It is also possible to get ski sticks with **hand-guards** over the handles, much like the hilt of a sword.

Shin pads are also available, some of which extend over the knee, and **head-guards** have become popular in recent years. The two most commonly-used types are the Happy Head, made by the Italian hat manufacturer, Conte of Florence, which is a foam rubber helmet with a hard plastic peak which protrudes over the forehead and deflects the poles before they can reach your face; and the **face-guard** made by the Japanese manufacturer, Conquest, which simply consists of a one-inch-thick plastic bar in front of the face at the level of the mouth. Some racers even use both together. **Slalom pants**

British Ski Federation

Ingemar Stenmark in Slalom. and **slalom sweaters** are well padded on the thighs, knees, shins and arms, but are very expensive and not worth using on plastic slopes as they are easily damaged if you fall.

Because the skis pass so close to the poles in Slalom, it is a common mistake to catch a tip or straddle a gate, when the tip of the inside ski goes just on the wrong side of the pole. To lessen the risk of this happening, **tip deflectors** can be fitted on to the tips of the skis; they are shaped like curved parrots' beaks, pointing inwards, and can knock against the pole and push the ski back into its correct position, although this will only happen in the really marginal cases.

In Giant Slalom, most young racers wear similar gear to that used for Slalom, but at the top levels of racing, the speeds are higher, and all racers wear either skintight **Downhill suits** or **GS suits**, which are like Downhill suits but with padding on the arms and legs for protection from the poles.

Downhill suits are skintight and stretchy, but they are no longer made from rubber, which was dangerous for two reasons: after a crash, the friction of the suit against the snow was so negligible that the racer would keep sliding on his back for great distances at high speed, and, the skin was unable to breathe. Nowadays, all suits are made from a Lycra material, and must let through a certain amount of air per square centimetre. Each suit is tested for this ability by FIS before being officially registered and acceptable.

Super Giant Slalom and Downhill are the fastest disciplines and all racers have to wear **helmets**. These are made with a hard exterior, unlike Slalom helmets, and are heavier than ice-hockey helmets but lighter than motorcycle helmets. It is up to each racer whether he wants to have a face-guard on the front.

The **ski sticks** used in Downhill are slightly curved, to fit more easily around the body and enable the racer to keep his elbows in, in line with his knees, when in the aerodynamic tuck position.

Martin Bell negotiating a high-speed turn in a Downhill.

One recent piece of equipment which has

The Draumbuie Liqueur Company

become very fashionable amongst racers, especially in Giant Slalom, is the **Derbyflex**, a metal plate with a layer of rubber beneath it, attached to the ski by screws at either end. The bindings are then mounted on to this plate, allowing the rubber layer to become a kind of shock absorber. As the screws at one end are able to move in a lengthwise direction, relative to the metal plate, the Derbyflex allows the ski to flex in to reverse camber more freely than with normally mounted bindings, where the toepiece, boot sole and heelpiece make up a stiff straight line which tends to block the flexing of the ski.

The Derbyflex undoubtedly makes a slight difference to the ski's performance, but this is only noticeable when a top racer is really putting maximum stress on the ski (e.g. in a fast, rough and icy Giant Slalom). For that reason it will probably never catch on with the recreational skier, and in any case the ski and binding manufacturers are already building features into their products which will perform the same function as the Derbyflex and possibly render it obsolete, at least as a separate unit ' fitted between ski and binding.

A piece of equipment fitted between ski and binding which has been with us for many more years than the Derbyflex, is the **wedge**. These are used (not only by racers) to compensate for bow-legs or knock-knees. Special long screws, which will go through the wedge and in to the ski, are necessary for the bindings. I once learnt this to my cost when I borrowed a pair of bindings from a friend who used wedges and drilled one of the screws right out through the base of the ski!

If the bow-legs or knock-knees are not too serious, it is sometimes easier to buy a pair of racing boots, which usually have a canting system. By adjusting a screw at the side of the ankle, the angle of the ankle is changed to compensate for the extra angle caused by the bow-legs or knock-knees. If you are bow-legged and do not use wedges or canting, when you stand in a normal position on your skis you will find yourself on your outside edges, (and on your inside edges if you are knock-kneed). Most ski-shop staff are trained to advise you in this matter.

EQUIPMENT FOR EXTREME COLD

When the air temperature drops below –15°C, it becomes very difficult to ski for a complete morning or afternoon without taking a break in the nearest mountain restaurant every hour or so. When the temperature approaches –25°C, it is only really possible to ski for half an hour at a time, with ten-minute breaks in a café to warm up. But there are certain extra pieces of equipment which will enable you to extend your skiing time and get maximum enjoyment from the snow, which at those temperatures will probably be light and powdery.

It goes without saying that you should have a good quality, well-insulated **ski suit**, with plenty of layers of clothing underneath, including thermal underwear. (It is a well-known fact that two thin layers of clothing are warmer than one thick one.) But the extremities of the body (feet, hands, face)

Martin Bell on a cold day, wearing a neoprene face mask.

The Drambuie Liqueur Company

will be the first to feel the cold and the longer you can keep these areas warm, the longer you will be able to ski.

Neoprene **face masks** are now available in Britain, manufactured by Whittaker Ltd, and if worn with a **hat** and **goggles** they will cover the whole face apart from a small hole around the mouth for breathing.

For the hands, **mittens** are warmer than **gloves**, and if you want extra warmth it is possible to get **handwarmers**. These come in different types: some are in airtight packets and react irreversibly with the air when opened, to produce heat; some can be used over and over again by boiling them up each evening and are triggered off by a metal catalyst. Most types are fairly effective, but it is inconvenient to carry enough handwarmers for a whole day, and so they are no substitute for a good pair of gloves.

To ensure that your feet remain warm, you have to first ensure that your boots are completely **Always start your day's** dry when you start your day's skiing. **skiing with dry boots** Most hotels dissuade guests from taking their boots up to their rooms by providing a **boot-room** where all the boots can be stored overnight. But unless this room is very warm and dry, I would advise most guests to carry their boots (unobtrusively) up to their room and leave them on the radiator overnight. The maid will never find out, as she will be cleaning your room during the morning while you are out skiing, and if hotel staff see you carrying your boots up to your room when you return from skiing, they will usually turn a blind eye as long as the boots are not covered in mud or slush. If the hotel staff do make a fuss, honesty is the best policy; tell them that your boots are wet and that the hotel's boot-room is not warm enough and, as often as not, they will befriend you and let you leave them somewhere warm, like the hotel laundry. It is really important that you start the day with a pair of boots which have plenty of heat stored within them, as this will give the blood circulation in your feet a chance to accustom itself to the tight fit of the boots before having to accustom itself to the cold. It goes without saying that your socks must be dry, and clean socks will keep your feet warm for longer than a sweaty, sticky old pair. There are **insoles** available which have a lining of silver foil on the underside, to reflect the cold back down, and these seem to have some effect. In the colder areas of North America it is possible to get boot covers made from waterproof material; they keep the snow off the surface of the boot, helping it to lose heat less quickly.

Once your boots have lost their stored heat, it is inevitable that you will have to come into a mountain restaurant to warm them up again. To do this quickly, you can put your boots on top of a radiator for a while, but if it is a cold day the radiator will probably already be covered with other people's stuff. So a really useful trick is to bring a hairdryer up in your rucksack, find a power point and blow hot air into your boots for a couple of minutes. If you can remove the inner boot, you will get the best result by blowing hot air into the shell of the boot (without the inner boot), as this is the part of the boot which stores the most heat. The hairdryer will also be useful for warming up your gloves. North American mountain restaurants have **warming machines** which will blow hot air into your boots or gloves if you put in a coin, but they do not give you very much time and there is often a queue for their use on a cold day, which will also be the case with the hand dryers in the toilets.

If after all these precautions you are still too cold, perhaps it is one of those days which you simply have to write off as being too cold for skiing. If your hotel has a sauna or heated swimming pool, that would be a better place to spend the afternoon.

3 SKIING

The four disciplines of Alpine racing mentioned in the last chapter are not the only types of skiing competition, and there are also many other recreational activities which people participate in on the slopes, apart from basic Alpine skiing. Some of these can even be done in the summer, whereas others are simply a way of doing something a little different during your winter ski holiday.

SUMMER SKIING

There are roughly between ten and twenty ski areas which remain open for most, if not all, of the summer and autumn months, benefiting from glaciers, some of which are massive rivers of ice, some of which are little more than large accumulations of snow which last only until about July.

There are summer ski areas in all of the main Alpine countries (Austria, Switzerland, Italy and France) and in general they are spread along the main central ridge of the Alps where the mountains are at their highest.

The term **glacier skiing** is actually somewhat misleading, as the skiing is always done on old snow which has remained since the previous winter, kept in place by the refrigerating effect of the ice of the glacier below. In fact, when the snow does melt away completely and the blue ice beneath is exposed, skiing becomes virtually impossible, partly because of the slipperiness of the surface (even for the sharpest edges), and partly because the ice contains small pieces of grit and rock which

The Draumbuie Liqueur Company

can ruin a pair of skis very quickly.

During earlier centuries, while the glaciers were being built up, the blue ice of the glacier was probably never exposed, as the winters produced more snow than the summer sun was capable of melting. But in recent years the climate has definitely become warmer and the glaciers are shrinking. In other words, each summer the sun is not only able to melt all the snow that was piled up during the previous winter, but is also able to melt some of the blue ice of the glacier once it is uncovered. Although it is quite possible to get snowfalls at these altitudes even in the middle of summer, they are usually mere sprinkles which evaporate as soon as the sun reappears. The lowest ebb of the glaciers usually occurs in late August and early September, when you have to look quite hard to find a decent patch of snow to ski on. The glaciers may be shrinking, but they are shrinking from the bottom upwards, and on the higher reaches of most large summer ski areas there are certain regions which always have ample snow cover.

If the weather is stable and the skies are clear,

The glacier at Tignes, France, in mid-summer. The village is just visible far below.

the snow will quickly become wet and slushy during the afternoons, but the temperature will always drop low enough overnight to freeze the snow into rock-hard ice. It is very important that the lift company prepares the *pistes* late each afternoon to provide a smooth surface for the next morning, otherwise all the small uneven areas which were innocuous piles of slush the previous day, will have been transformed into hard lumps of ice capable of overturning a skier. But if the *pistes* have been prepared, the frozen slush is not too difficult to ski on, and by ten or eleven o'clock the increasing power of the sun will have melted and softened the top few inches of the snow, producing a surface which is firm yet easy to grip. These enjoyable conditions are known as **spring snow**. Later on, around twelve or one o'clock, the snow becomes too slushy for enjoyment and the lifts close down.

The worst conditions for summer skiing are when the weather remains cloudy overnight, but it is not cold enough to snow. The cloud cover acts as an insulating layer, trapping the heat of the day and preventing the temperatures from dropping low enough to freeze the snow. It will then be slushy for all the following morning.

National ski teams of many countries make great use of glaciers for their training. This is because **Many national ski teams** there is little time between races dur- **regularly train on glaciers** ing the winter to do extensive training, and certainly no time to make basic changes to technique. So in the summer, and even more so in the autumn, there will be periods when there will actually be more racers skiing on the glacier than normal skiers. One method of combatting the slushy conditions created by overcast weather was discovered by ski teams on glaciers several years ago: spreading coarse salt (as used to clear roads in winter) or fertilizer on to the snow, just in the immediate area of the Slalom or Giant Slalom course which was to be used, would lower the temperature of the snow for several hours. This produced a nice hard surface which would not develop ruts or holes and could be used for a long time before the course had to be changed. However, it was recently discovered that the use of **snow cement**, as this process became known, contributed in the long term towards the shrinking of the glaciers. Quite apart from that, the chemicals were draining off the glacier and getting into the drinking water of the valleys below. So now snow cement has been banned from almost all glaciers, and racers simply have to put up with slush when they encounter it. The process is still allowed, however, for actual races held on lower, non-glacier slopes during the winter, and it is very useful for late-season races in March and April.

Several factors will help you to decide which glacier to go to, if you feel the desperate urge to do some skiing in the summer or autumn. The first is obviously the size of the glacier: it can become very boring spending a week skiing up and down one lift. Hintertux and Sölden in Austria, Zermatt and Saas Fee in Switzerland, and Tignes in France, are acknowledged to be the largest ski areas. The second deciding factor is the amount of work done by the lift company in preparing the *pistes*, for the reasons mentioned earlier. There is no official information available on this subject and you will probably have to rely upon word-of-mouth from other skiers. Although every summer ski area is different and it is impossible to generalize, it is often said that lift companies in Austria and Switzerland are more conscientious than those in France and Italy when it comes to preparing the *pistes*. Many of the Italian glaciers, however, are in the South Tyrol, where the Austrian attitude prevails.

There are many different means of access to the glaciers from the villages which serve them. Some of these villages are themselves already at quite a high altitude (right at the top end of the valley where the road ends), whereas others are lower, but it will usually take a long time to travel up to the skiing in the mornings, so you have to get up very early to get the best of the conditions.

The most convenient way to travel up is on a gondola like in Hintertux or Tignes, as it is comfortable and fairly quick. Some glaciers, like Kaprun or Pitztal, have funiculars, which are very fast but can be crowded and uncomfortable at busy times. Cable-cars, which are the means of access to the Zermatt glacier, can also be uncomfortable and are slower than funiculars. Sölden and Kaunertal are among the glaciers which have direct road access right up to the snowline, which is very comfortable, convenient and fast (if you have a powerful car), but there are extra expenses in the form of petrol and wear and tear on the vehicle, which often has to be thrashed up steep hills for long periods in a low gear. If you are on a coach holiday this is fine, but if you have travelled out to the Alps by other means and do not have a car, you will become dependent on inflexible bus schedules.

You will also want to avoid long queues as much as possible, and there are a couple of facts which will help you do this: smaller glaciers are less busy than large ones; the French prefer to ski in the summer (during school holidays) rather than in the autumn, whereas the Germans prefer to ski (in Austria) during the autumn, especially during the 'potato-picking holidays' in early October and the All Saints' Day holidays at the beginning of November.

GRASS SKIING

Grass skiing started during the 1970s in Europe, and the basic design of a grass ski has not changed much since then, although refinements have been made in order to produce added speed for grass ski racers. The grass ski is about 80 centimetres long, operating on the principle of a caterpillar-track, not unlike a smaller version of those used on earth-moving machinery. This track runs on rollers around a static frame, to which a platform for the boot and binding is attached.

The grass ski is not designed to skid sideways on the grass, but has a slight bend (similar to reverse

camber on a normal ski) enabling carved turns to be made.

Because of this, grass skiing is an excellent way for recreational skiers to improve their technique, especially when used in conjunction with dry ski slopes, as the skills taught by the two surfaces complement each other well and should produce a better snow skier the following winter. It is even more important for young racers who cannot get enough skiing on snow, to race on grass skis as well as on dry ski slopes. The former will teach them what a carved turn should feel like and how to improve their line taken down the course by

Martin Bell competing in the World Grass Ski Championships.

turning above the gates (not once they reach them); the latter will teach them how to hold an edge on a slippery surface and how to produce speed by the use of stepped turns.

There are, so far, only a few grass ski centres in Britain, where you can hire grass skis and get instruction, but a complete list of these centres is available from the governing body, the **British National Grass Ski Congress**. They can also supply you with a calendar of all the grass ski races, which are held fairly regularly through the summer at the various centres. (*See* Chapter 7 for address.)

Grass skiing becomes more difficult when the turf becomes damp, because the previous racers will have churned up the surface and made it muddy and slippery. A skid on grass skis is very difficult to correct, but it is excellent balance training and will prepare you for icy conditions on snow.

The limiting factor in grass skiing is the design of the skis; they will only get up to a certain speed before their internal friction becomes too great and they will go no faster. Because of this, Giant Slaloms and Super Giant Slaloms, although feasible on grass (unlike on most dry slopes), produce lower speeds than their equivalents on snow, and Downhills are not possible. Many top grass ski-racers have actually developed metal-workers' skills through the amount of changes which they make to their grass skis to make them faster, and unfortunately many grass ski Giant and Super Giant Slaloms are decided in the workshop and not by the racers' skills. But Slaloms are as fast as those on snow, and just as much skill is required. Moreover, grass ski Slaloms are usually held on longer and more interesting terrain than Slaloms on dry slopes, all of which helps the education of a young ski racer.

ALPINE RACING AND RULES

The four disciplines of Alpine racing have already been mentioned in previous chapters. To remind you, in a list with the fastest and longest first, they are Downhill, Super Giant Slalom, Giant Slalom and

Slalom. Super Giant Slalom is often abbreviated to Super G; Giant Slalom to GS.

These disciplines form the main basis for most kinds of competitions on skis, from a basic dry slope race (e.g. an inter-school competition), right up to the World Cup, World Championships and Olympic Games. Indeed, even if your only experience of racing has been the end-of-week race organized by a Ski School in the Alps, when the instructors set a time and everyone is awarded gold, silver and bronze medals depending on how far behind they are, you have probably already skied a simple GS.

Back in the 1920s, when the pastime of sliding down hills on a pair of planks was only just becoming popular, especially in the Alps, the only acknowledged forms of ski competition were cross-country racing and ski-jumping. These disciplines had originated in Norway, where skiing was first invented many centuries ago, and were based on Scandinavia's relatively flat terrain and had evolved from what was originally merely a way of getting around through the endless snowclad forests. There were no official competitions which took advantage of the Alps' far greater vertical drop, and so the pioneers of skiing in the Alps invented a couple: Downhill, which in those days consisted simply of a start gate at the top of the mountain and a finish gate at the bottom (the racer had to choose as fast a route as his skill or courage would allow); and Slalom, where the racer had to turn through gates marked by wooden poles, presumably inspired by the problems encountered when skiing through trees.

The Englishman, Arnold Lunn, was probably the most forceful amongst these pioneers in persuading the organizers of major events such as the Winter Olympic Games to allow the new disciplines to feature alongside the established ones of cross-country and ski-jumping. When this was finally achieved, the new disciplines were known as the Alpine events after their region of origin, and cross-

Allsport/Bob Martin

Alberto Tomba in a Slalom. country and ski-jumping became known as the Nordic events after theirs. Not long after this, the new discipline of Giant Slalom was introduced, as a kind of Downhill with control gates to keep the speed lower. The next addition then came only seven years ago, when FIS realized that the Giant Slaloms had become more turny and slower over the years, until they resembled Slalom far more closely than Downhill, although originally it had been intended as a kind of halfway house between the two. As a consequence, racers were either specializing in Downhill, or the other two technical disciplines, and virtually no-one was competing in all three any more. The fourth discipline, Super G, was created as a halfway house between GS and Downhill, to encourage racers to try to excel at more disciplines.

The course dimensions of all four disciplines are strictly laid down in the FIS rules, from the minimum and maximum distances permitted between the gates, to the recommended vertical drop (which is obviously smallest for Slalom and largest for Downhill). In Slalom and GS, the course must contain a certain number of gates (give or take a few), depending on the vertical drop of the run on which the course is set. In Downhill, more freedom is given to the course-setter, as the course is not constantly turning like the technical events, and there are always a few straight sections. Such a section of the course is known as a **Schuss**, from the German word for shot, which is appropriate because the racers try to make themselves as aerodynamic as possible, when negotiating a *Schuss*, and crouch down in a bullet-like position. Super G is also defined by a set of dimensions, but as it is such a young discipline there are still many different interpretations of these rules, and many different Super G courses.

As a rough guide, Slaloms are usually between 40 seconds and 1 minute long, Giant Slaloms between 55 seconds and 1 minute 25 seconds, Super Gs between 1 minute 20 seconds and 1 minute 50 seconds, and Downhills between 1 minute 20 seconds and 2 minutes 10 seconds long. The average speeds are approximately 25 mph for Slalom, 35 mph for GS, 45 mph for Super G, and 60 mph for Downhill (although on some parts of the course it can reach 90 mph).

The period before the start of a race, when the racers are allowed to look at the course and memorize it, is known as the **inspection**. In Downhill, Super G and GS, this is done by side-slipping slowly down the course (but not skiing through it); in Slalom, the racers must walk up the course, wearing their skis (otherwise their boots would leave holes in the snow). This is because a racer who is side-slipping fairly briskly down a Slalom is not travelling much more slowly than when he races through it (tantamount to practising on the course), and a Slalom course is so short that it does not require too much effort to walk up it.

In Downhill, in addition to the inspection, official **training runs** are held on the exact course which will be used for the race, for the preceding three (sometimes two) days. A training run is organized

The Drambuie Liqueur Company

Graham Bell negotiating a Downhill jump. in the same way as the race, with all the racers starting in their usual order at 40 second intervals, and it is usually timed. The results of the training runs have no official meaning, although some teams will undoubtedly use them for internal qualifications. (For example, only ten Austrians are allowed to enter a World Cup Downhill, but four-teen may be allowed to participate in the training runs, with the slowest four then having to drop out on race day.)

Either one or two training runs are held each day, so, weather permitting, a maximum of six could theoretically be held, although the usual number is five, as only one run is held on the final day of training, in order to give the race organizers extra time to repair the ruts left by the racers in training and to get the course into good shape for the race. It also gives the racers a little extra rest before race day.

But even if bad weather disrupts the programme, a minimum of two training runs must be held. If necessary, they will even hold a training run on the morning of the race. Anyone who wishes to race must have participated in at least one training run. This rule reflects the whole purpose of training runs in Downhill, which is to allow racers to get to know the course in as safe a way as possible. There are usually three inspections, one on each day of training, and none on the morning of the race (unless the conditions have changed dramatically overnight).

The start list is decided on the basis of British Seed Points (or FIS points for international races), with the best going first. However the fifteen best racers are all put into a hat and drawn for the first fifteen start numbers at random.

This is done for all races on snow, to give the better racers the advantage of smoother and less rutted snow conditions. In Downhills, **All courses are checked by forerunners** Super Gs or GSs, if there has been **just before the race begins** an exceptional amount of new snow overnight, the organizers are obliged to provide six extra **fore-runners** (skiers who ski down the course just before the race begins). In races in all disciplines, at least three forerunners are sent down to check that the course is acceptable and that the electronic timing is functioning, and to remove any excess soft snow from the racing line. But in

The Drambuie Liqueur Company

Downhill, and occasionally in GS or Super G, there is often so much snow after an overnight fall that it cannot all be removed from the course. If there were still only three forerunners, they would not remove or pack down the snow enough, and the first few racers from the first fifteen would be at a disadvantage, as a faster track would not yet be formed. If the organizers cannot find six competent skiers (who are not already entered in the race) to act as extra forerunners, then six racers are drawn at random from the last 20 per cent of the field, and sent down before the first fifteen (but after the usual three forerunners), and are known as the snow seed, powder seed or snowplough. Although they will be slowed down by the deep new snow, they will encounter far smoother conditions than usual, and it is sometimes a chance for youngsters to achieve a breakthrough.

All racers are then issued with **bibs** showing their number, which they must wear, with the number visible, whenever they are competing or inspecting the course (so that they can be identified if they, for example, side-slip down a Slalom course, an offence which will lead to a warning then disqualification). If a bib is too baggy and not aerodynamic enough, extra knots may be tied in it to make it tighter, but the racer is not allowed to tighten it with tape, thread, or safety pins.

Once the course has been set, the inspection will take place, lasting between 45 minutes and 1 hour. Then 15 minutes will be allowed for clearing everyone off the course, and for any last-minute preparations to the course. In the technical events this will include sliding any excess soft snow off the course, and in the high-speed events (Super G and Downhill) the race officials may decide to sprinkle **pine needles** on to the snow if there is poor visibility through mist, shade or flat light. The needles are soft enough not to do any damage to racers' skis, but dark enough to give some contrast to the snow and help the racers to orientate themselves. If it is snowing hard, it is especially important to put the pine needles down at the last minute, otherwise they will be covered by snow before the race even starts.

Once the race gets underway, it is up to every racer to get himself to the start on time. If you are late for your start, the official in charge of the start (the **Start Referee**) is empowered to let you start only if your delay was caused by *force*

Opposite:
The British Ski Team physio massages Graham Bell's legs to warm them up, a few minutes before he is due to start his race. His skis and bindings will have been checked by technicians, and he has already removed his outer, warmer clothing.

majeure (i.e. something beyond your control). This may include the breakdown of one of the lifts, or the absence of a large number of preceding racers, but may not include personal equipment failure (for example, if your boot buckle breaks and you have to spend time getting it fixed), or minor illness (e.g. sickness or diarrhoea).

Once the racer has got himself into the **start gate** on time, he has to pay attention to the start signal which will indicate when he has to go. The actual electronic clock which will time his run will be started when he opens the start gate, a thin horizontal rod or wand at shin height, attached, via a hinge at one end, to a stake in the ground. The hinge contains a switch which will start the clock. But the racer must leave the start gate within a prescribed time limit. In Downhill, Super G, and GS there are fixed **start intervals**, no less than 40 seconds and no more than 90 seconds. The racer must leave the start gate within the limits of 3 seconds before or 3 seconds after the official start time. If he starts more than 3 seconds before his designated time, the racer will be disqualified. The times for racers starting more than 3 seconds after their official start time will be calculated as if they had started exactly 3 seconds after their start time. So if a racer starts 4 seconds after his official start time he will effectively have a 1 second penalty added on to the actual time which he takes to ski down the course. The racer will be given a 10-second warning before his start time, and will then be given the start command '5–4–3–2–1–Go'. Instead of this, if possible, an audible start signal is often used, in conjunction with a visible clock.

In Slalom, there are no fixed start intervals, as there are sometimes many slalom poles to be replaced and the next racer cannot go until the mess created by the previous racer has been cleared up. When this has been done, the starter will give the command 'Ready . . . Go'; if the racer does not start within 10 seconds after this command he will be disqualified.

The racer must have both his ski sticks planted in the snow in front of the wand before he starts, and he is not allowed to use the start gate or start hut to push off from.

Once on the course, the racer has to ski through every gate on the course; the tips of his skis and his boots have to pass through each gate, or round the point in the snow where the gate would be (if the pole has been knocked out of its vertical position by another part of the racer's body). The gates are alternately blue and red, except for Downhill, when they are all red. In Slalom, a gate consists of two single poles of the same colour, between 4 and 6 metres apart. In GS, Super G and Downhill, a gate is made up by two pairs of poles of the same colour, each pair with a coloured flag (approximately 75 centimetres wide) tied between them. The gate through which the racer has to ski is then between the two pairs of flags, which are in GS 4 – 8 metres apart, in Super G 6 – 8 metres apart, and in Downhill at least 8 metres apart.

There are **gatekeepers** spread along the course, usually with three gates each to supervise, whose duty it is to disqualify racers who fail to pass through any of the gates. If a racer crashes or makes any kind of error which causes him to stop, and he is not sure whether he has missed a gate, he can ask the gatekeeper, who must tell him to go on, if he has not missed any gates, or to go back if he has. Any racer who receives outside help of any kind during his run will be disqualified. This includes advice on whether to go back because of a missed gate, or help with replacing a ski after a crash.

Any racer who continues to ski the course in a Downhill after falling or being overtaken by another racer and any racer who misses two or more gates in a row but then re-enters the course and continues to ski down it (except in Downhill), will be given an oral or written reprimand, or will be suspended from the next discipline at that event or from any FIS event for the next seven days.

A racer is allowed to stop his run and claim a **re-run** (another chance to ski down the course as soon as he has got back up to the start), if he is hindered by any of the following things: an official, a spectator, an animal, a fallen competitor (or, in Downhill, a yellow flag warning of a fallen competitor), equipment such as a ski or ski stick left by a previous competitor, the first aid service, or the absence of a gate knocked out by a previous competitor. The claim for a re-run can only be made in any of these cases if the racer leaves the course immediately upon being hindered. If the claim is proved to be unfounded, the racer will be disqualified. If a racer reaches the finish but is then not given a time because of a malfunctioning of the timing equipment, a re-run is also allowed.

If a racer feels that he has been unjustly **disqualified**, he has 15 minutes after the announcement of the disqualification at the end of the run in which to protest. He should get his trainer or team manager to do this for him and a deposit of 100 Swiss Francs must be made, which will only be returned if the protest is successful (to stop speculative protesting). These rules only count in international races and in less important races it is acceptable for a racer to make a protest on his own behalf.

The most common cause of contention is the **straddle**, when one of the tips of the racer's skis passes just on the wrong side of the pole, which then passes between the racer's legs. This is not as painful as it sounds, because the modern hinged poles bend down very quickly, as soon as they are knocked by the edge of the ski or the racer's shin. For the same reason, it is very difficult for the untrained eye to notice a straddle, and it is only evident from the way it splits a racer's feet slightly and throws him off balance. However, in a similar fashion to American Football (but not cricket, football or tennis), the officials' job is made easier by being allowed to study action replays on video. All World Cups are televised, and nowadays there is someone with a portable video camera at most races.

It has already been noted that the racer must pass through each gate with both ski tips and both feet, but the one exception to this rule is when the racer has already lost a ski further up the course and is attempting to continue on one ski. He must be wearing at least one ski while he negotiates the further gates and skis through the finish, unless he loses his second ski in a crash just before the finish and slides across the line.

In Downhill the rules are slightly different: the racer must be wearing both skis when he skis through all the gates. If he falls or loses a ski he must not re-commence his run. But he is allowed to cross the finish line wearing one or no skis, provided the ski or skis were lost in a crash just before the finish and he slides across the line.

AMATEURS AND PROFESSIONALS

Alpine racing has been part of the Winter Olympic Games since 1936 and has usually been regarded as an amateur sport. In fact, the great Austrian skier, Karl Schranz, was sent home in disgrace from the 1972 Games because it was discovered that he had appeared in an advertisement for a brand of mustard.

But recently, sports administrators have begun to realize that amateurism was, in reality, an invention of the British upper classes in the nineteenth century, designed to prevent the working classes from competing with them on equal terms; to be at all successful at any sport, you have to devote a lot of time to it, which is difficult when you have a full-time job but easy when you are living from the interest on substantial savings.

Moreover, some countries, especially those of the Eastern Bloc, began to pay their athletes for being theoretical employees of Government agencies (such as the police or customs officers), when in fact they were allowed to spend most of their time training.

Facing up to these realities, the International Olympic Committee has allowed any sports to be considered as possible Olympic sports, even fully professional ones such as tennis, so long as no money is paid for the competitors' actual participation in the Games. The regulations for all other **Advertising patches are strictly** competitions are decided by the **regulated by FIS** governing body for that particular sport, and in 1985 FIS relaxed the rules slightly, allowing two extra **advertising patches** on the skiers' equipment, other than only the name of the manufacturers of the equipment, which was previously the case.

Hardware (skis, boots, bindings, ski sticks etc.) must carry the names or trademarks of the company which actually produces that item of equipment, and the brandings must be the same as on products sold to the public.

Martin Bell with several sponsors' logos visible. (The Drambuie sticker on the ski is not permitted and was removed before the competition.)

Gloves and goggles may only carry the name or logo of the company which actually produces them, and the branding should not be larger than 6 square centimetres.

Any article of clothing may only carry two commercial markings: one can belong to the manu-

The Drambuie Liqueur Company

facturer of the garment and the other to a separate team sponsor, or, if the national governing body so chooses, both may belong either to the manufacturer or to the separate team sponsor. Only one national team sponsor is allowed per country, except when the Men's Team and the Women's Team each have a separate sponsor. Each marking should be no larger than 30 square centimetres, and the two markings are not allowed to appear one above the other or one beside the other. The name or logo of the national team sponsor is not allowed to appear more than twice on a competitor's clothing at any given time.

Each helmet or item of headgear is allowed to carry two markings, of 6 square centimetres each, belonging to the manufacturer of the headgear, one over each ear. In addition, there is a space of 30 square centimetres on the helmet or headgear which may be used by a separate sponsor. It is up to the national governing body whether this space is used by one team sponsor or by different sponsors for individual racers. In any case, the front of the helmet or headgear must carry the emblem of the national team, and the advertising must be at least 2 centimetres distant from this emblem.

Individual skiers are not allowed to sign contracts with sponsors; the contract must be between the national governing body and the sponsor, with the money being paid into a fund held on the skier's behalf by the governing body. The skier is allowed access to this fund to cover accommodation costs, and travel costs to training and competition sites. The skier is also allowed to be paid compensation for loss of income (i.e. the income he would have received had he not been a full-time ski-racer), the amount to be decided by the national governing body.

In the case of Britain, the national governing body which is authorized to make these decisions is the British Ski Federation.

There is, however, a fully **professional circuit** which has been in existence since the early 1970s, based on parallel slalom racing. This is done in knockout format, starting with thirty-two racers. There are always more than this number entered in the race and so two qualification runs are held, against the clock, just like an amateur slalom. The fastest sixteen from the first run qualify automatically for the knockout stage and do not have to do a second run; the fastest sixteen from the second run go through to join them. The seeding is then based on the times in the qualifying rounds.

As the two parallel courses can never be completely identical, each race is held over two runs, with the racers swapping courses. An electronic timing beam at the finish measures the difference between the racers on each run, and the faster racer in total goes through to the next round. A certain amount of tactics come into play, for if you have managed to get a one-second lead after the first run, all you need do on the second run is keep him in your sights, ski reliably and not make any mistakes. The starting technique required is also different, as both racers have to start on the command of 'go'. There are thick metal gates (similar in shape to the swing-doors of old-fashioned Western saloons), which do not open until the start command is given.

Although the format of professional racing requires very good fitness (to win you may have to do ten races in one day), many of the pros are older racers who have retired from amateur racing. Pro racing is not recognized by FIS, and under the present rules there is no going back to amateur racing once you have turned professional.

Ironically, the top pros do not earn as much as the top amateurs (Olympic Champions, World Champions), even though the latter get no prize money and must make all their money through endorsements of ski equipment and the helmet sponsors. But the amateurs must get permission from their national ski association for any contract they sign, and often have to pay a certain percentage levy to the association, whereas the pros have total freedom to sign contracts with sponsors and may carry as much advertising on their equipment as they choose.

The pro circuit is now getting richer each year and is based mainly in North America. The American spectators are not as knowledgeable about ski-racing as the Austrian, Swiss or Italian crowds, and they find the head-to-head format easier to understand. There is also a satellite circuit in Japan, and once a season the best racers on the American tour are flown over to Japan to race the best of the Japanese tour.

Recently the Mahre twins (Phil and Steve) made a comeback to ski-racing and joined the pro tour. It was four years since they had retired after winning Gold and Silver medals in the Slalom at the 1984 Olympics, and they did no better or worse than expected: they were not completely out of touch, nor did they sweep the board in everything. It showed that the pro tour is now no longer a Mickey Mouse event, and, in my opinion, the best pro racer could certainly score consistent top ten placings in World Cup Slaloms, although it must be said that the two formats require racers with different mental approaches. Some racers who were only mediocre amateur racers have dominated the pro circuit, while big names from World Cup Slalom have often failed to make the adjustment to parallel slalom racing.

There is a variation of parallel slalom racing which is often demonstrated on dry slopes in Britain, but which I have never seen being done at a high level on snow. This is the **team parallel relay**, usually with four members per team. The first member of each team sets off when given the start command, as in any parallel slalom. Then, when the first member of the team crosses the finish line, an electronic sound signal is sent to the start, informing the next member of the team that he can start, and so on until the last member of the team reaches the finish. The first team to get all its members to the finish is the winner and progresses through to the next round in the usual manner.

Teams are usually formed from regions of Britain, the Home Nations, or clubs, and the racing is often exciting to watch.

SPEED SKIING

The sport of **speed skiing** developed on the Kleine Matterhorn glacier, right on the Italian/Swiss border and high above the villages of Zermatt and Cervinia. Originally the competition was known as the *Kilometro Lanciato*, or Flying Kilometre.

The course at Cervinia was dead straight, but the skiers had to jump over a crevasse near the top, when their speed was still relatively low, in order to be on the right line to get the maximum acceleration from the long steep pitch below. The whole course was roughly 1,000 metres long (hence the name) but the timing was only measured over a

A speed skier in an aerodynamic tuck, complete with moulded helmet and rubberized suit.

Bob Thomas Sports Photography

100 metre section near the bottom, at the point of maximum speed. The course also had the advantage of being at high altitude: the thinner air meant less wind resistance.

Since the beginnings of the sport in the early 1960s, the speeds attained have become higher and higher, and the current world record is 131 mph, held by Michel Pruefer of France. During the 1970s, the KL was banned from the Kleine Matterhorn glacier when jurisdiction over the area passed from the Italians to the Swiss after a border revision. The Zermatt authorities ruled that the course, in particular the **compression** at the bottom, was too dangerous to be used any more. A compression is a part of the course, often found in Downhill, where the terrain changes from very steep to very flat, abruptly. The roller-coaster effect caused by this can exert downwards forces of several g's through the skier, and legs which are not strong enough will simply collapse and give way.

Since then, the speed-skiing organizers have chosen safer slopes on which to prepare courses, with a gradient which starts off very steeply and then gradually flattens out towards the bottom. After Cervinia, the main speed-skiing competitions were held at Portillo, in Chile, where the current record was set, but the world records have also been broken at Les Arcs, in France.

Apart from the courage needed to hold an aerodynamic position at high speed, when even the smoothly-prepared speed-skiing tracks feel bumpy, there is less skill involved than in the established forms of Alpine ski-racing, because there are no turns to be negotiated. For this reason, the speed-skiers can use skis which are very stable at high speeds and are not designed to turn, 240 centimetres in length and with virtually no sidecut. There are even competitions held for recreational skiers at Les Arcs and, with a smooth enough course, some basic schooling in the correct position, and the right equipment, it is not unknown for a completely average skier to break 100 mph.

This is not to say that Downhillers cannot learn anything from speed-skiers. Many of the equipment refinements which they have made (such as egg-shaped helmets and polystyrene fins attached to the back of the calves to reduce turbulence) would not be practical in Downhill because they would restrict the mobility needed for turning and jumping. Rubberized suits, which are banned in Downhill, are acceptable in speed-skiing events, which are always held above the tree-line where there are no obstacles for the racer to collide with if he slides for great distances after a fall.

Speed-skiers have proved that although the aerodynamic tuck position with the hands held close to the face is superior at low speeds (60 – 70 mph), it is more stable at higher speeds to hold the hands lower and further forward. It has also been established in speed-skiing that larger bodies generally go faster in a straight line than smaller ones, mainly because the increase in surface area (which is proportional to the wind resistance slowing you down) is not as great as the increase in mass, or inertia, which is necessary to keep you going against the wind resistance. However, in Downhill it must be noted that increased weight is only beneficial if you have enough power-to-weight ratio to hold yourself in a good aerodynamic position against the g-forces in the turns and compressions.

Speed-skiing was originally professional, but in the mid-1980s it became amateur and came under the jurisdiction of FIS. It is not an Olympic sport, but at the 1992 Olympics it will be a demonstration sport, with the chance of being chosen as a full Olympic sport by 1994.

FREESTYLE

The origins of freestyle skiing were in a pastime known as **hot-dogging** during the mid-1970s, far later than the beginnings of speed-skiing, yet **freestyle** was the first to be brought under the auspices of FIS and therefore the first to gain Olympic credibility. In 1988, all three disciplines of freestyle (moguls,

Opposite:
Julia Snell, of the British Freestyle Team, performs a flip in ballet. Note the green hills and valley in the background – this shot was taken on a glacier during summer training.

British Ski Federation

aerials, and ballet) were demonstration sports at the Calgary Olympics. The moguls discipline has been accepted as a full Olympic sport for Albertville in 1992, while the other two disciplines will remain in the demonstration category for the time being.

The original hot-doggers were a bunch of ski bums at certain ski resorts in the USA, who were looking for a new way of expressing themselves and having fun. At first, this consisted of finding a steep run with massive moguls on it, and taking turns to see who could ski it in the wildest and most out-of-control manner. Then they started to do jumps off the larger bumps, doing acrobatics while in mid-air, and doing complicated twisting and stepping manoeuvres while on the ground. Later, this mish-mash of tricks was resolved into the three disciplines of freestyle: **moguls**, which involves skiing down a very steep bumps run; **aerials**, where the skier is launched from a specially-made jump and performs spectacular acrobatics in mid-air; and **ballet**, where fluent and graceful manoeuvres are linked together to the accompaniment of music, on a flat, smooth *piste*. The name hot-dogging has been dropped, as freestylers want to gain credibility for what is a very skilful sport, and play down its ski bum origins, but some of the original spirit remains in the German name for the sport, *Trickski*.

Moguls are so far the only discipline of freestyle to be accepted into the Olympic fold, probably because it is the only one where conventional skiing technique is required. The event begins with competitors skiing, one after the other, down a steep bumpy *piste* on which they will have had two days of training. The competitor's run, which is usually about 60 seconds long, is marked by five judges, and the composition of the marks is strictly defined. 25 per cent is based simply upon time: the faster the run, the better the marks. 25 per cent of the marks depend on the air which the skier achieves, in other words the two compulsory jumps which he has to perform during the run. Inverted manoeuvres (somersaults, etc.) are banned during moguls, because the landing is too difficult to achieve safely. Double helicopters (two full 360 degree revolutions in mid-air) are generally the most difficult jumps done in a mogul run. The other 50 per cent of the marks are given for the style of the skier (steady upper body and head, good turning of the skis across the fall-line, and enough flexion and extension of the knees to absorb the bumps), and the line taken (as many turns as possible in a straight line down the hill, with no traverses across the fall-line).

The best eight skiers from this qualifying stage go into the quarter-finals of a knockout stage, where the skiers ski head-to-head next to each other down the run. There are gates which they have to go through to make sure that they do not get in each other's way. It is a little misleading for the crowd, because the fastest run is not always the best, but usually the faster skier has gained that extra speed by taking a more direct line down the hill and will therefore also be marked more generously.

Because of the Olympic medals up for grabs in the moguls event at the 1992 Olympics in Albertville, many competent Slalom racers, who are used to making quick short turns anyway, will try to apply their skills to moguls.

Ballet is the discipline of freestyle which tries to model itself on figure skating as much as possible. As well as being acrobatic, the skier must appear artistic and graceful. The event is set to music chosen by the competitor as in the free programme in figure skating.

There are five judges, who give marks for two elements of the competitor's programme: artistic interpretation and technical difficulty. The most difficult moves (mainly those involving flips using the ski sticks) are given grades of technical difficulty, and the competitor must announce in advance which moves he is going to attempt.

The ballet programme of each competitor usually lasts about 2 minutes. The event is held on a smooth, flat slope which is a couple of hundred metres long and for this reason ballet is the only discipline of freestyle which can be practised on dry slopes in Britain. There are also ballet displays staged at events such as the London Ski Show, when temporary dry ski slopes are erected, using scaffolding, inside an exhibition hall.

The third discipline of freestyle, the **aerials**, is the most exciting to watch but is also the discipline which requires the least actual skiing technique. A 20 metre run-in is all that is needed to generate enough speed to catapult the skier into the air off a steep ramp which is carefully built from snow. After performing complicated somersaults and twists in the air, the skier lands on a steep ramp. The very sharp gradient serves to lessen the impact of landing, and the snow on the landing area is always kept soft, even if there are icy conditions elsewhere on the mountain.

Usually there is more than one actual jump built for a competition: there may be a straight ramp for forward somersaults, and a couple of kickers (ramps with an upwards curve) for back somersaults. There may be a large kicker for the actual competition, and a smaller one which the competitors can use to warm up on. Once the jumps have been constructed from snow, they are sprayed with water to harden them up in the overnight cold. The next day they will be solid ice and ready to withstand use by a large number of competitors.

There are five judges for aerials, who give marks for the following categories: 25 per cent for the take-off where the judges are looking for a pop, i.e. a sharp push with the legs, just as the skis are being bent into reverse camber by the curve of the kicker. This will give maximum height. 50 per cent is for the technical difficulty of the jump (triple somersaults with twists are often seen in competitions nowadays) and the amount of height attained. 25 per cent of the mark is for the landing, the neater the better. No part of the upper body is allowed to come into contact with the snow during the landing, so if the competitor falls or puts a hand down to steady himself, he will lose his landing marks and effectively be out of contention.

The aerials are dangerous and helmets are compulsory for all competitors. In 1985, Mike Nemesvary, Britain's top aerialist and one of the best in the world, suffered a broken neck and was paralysed whilst practising on a trampoline.

Aerials have a lot in common with the sports

of trampolining and diving. All three use similar moves, and it is even possible for a top trampolinist to learn the rudiments of skiing (for a controlled take-off and landing) and become a good aerialist very quickly. As well as using the trampoline, aerialists can practise when they are not on snow using Dendix jumps, with the landings in water or on an airbag. The latter can even be used for displays at exhibitions such as the London Ski Show.

The equipment used by freestylers is quite different from that used by racers. Very short skis are used in all disciplines, although less so in moguls, and long ski sticks are used in ballet to help the flips. Normal length sticks are used in moguls, whereas the aerialists use none at all.

NORDIC SKIING

The sport which is given the general name of Nordic skiing comprises, in fact, two basic activities: **cross-country** (often known by its German name of *Langlauf*) and **ski-jumping**.

Nordic skiing comprises cross-country skiing and ski-jumping

At Olympic, World Championship and World Cup levels there are individual cross-country events for men and women at several distances, the longest and most gruelling being the 50 kilometre marathon. In these events, skiers are sent off from the start at regular intervals and there is no actual head-to-head racing, although it is quite normal for a top skier to overtake several of the slower skiers ahead of him. There is plenty of width on the track to accommodate this.

Although cross-country skiing is basically a sport where the athlete must work to produce his own speed across the flat, on the circuits used for competitions there are always slight climbs, where the skiers have to work even harder, and slight descents, where the skiers have a chance to rest a little. They cannot let their concentration wander though, as the downhill sections often contain turns which have to be negotiated at relatively high speeds (20 or 30 mph). What makes these turns especially difficult is the nature of cross-country equipment. The skis are very narrow in order to be as light as possible, and the bindings only hold the foot at the toe, allowing the heel to lift up for more forward push on each step. The boots are very light and soft, more akin to running shoes than ski boots, and to make downhill skiing even harder there are no edges on the skis. The ski sticks used are similar to Alpine sticks, but slightly longer to give a more effective push.

The traditional, or diagonal, technique involves pushing straight forward off each ski alternately,

Cross-country skiing at a leisurely pace is a peaceful way to enjoy the winter scenery.

Tony Stone Worldwide/Paul Berger

just like running with skis on the feet. To allow this, the ski must be waxed with special sticky wax, known as *klister*, to stop it from slipping back whenever the skier pushes off from it.

Since the mid-1980s, a new cross-country technique has been developed by the top skiers, using skating steps in a similar way to ice-skating. FIS, who are the international governing body of Nordic skiing, soon came to terms with skating, and decreed that it could only be used in designated skating events. The traditional diagonal technique can only be used in designated diagonal events. There are now separate skating and diagonal races for all distances, very much along the same lines as the different strokes in swimming.

The reason for the segregation becomes clear when considering the types of track needed for the two techniques. The diagonal technique requires a track of two parallel grooves to keep the skis running straight and parallel, whereas skating simply requires a smooth surface; when skiers first started using the skating technique on traditional tracks, the grooves were filled in and the track was destroyed.

As well as the individual races already mentioned, there is a relay competition between national teams. Each team member does a 10 kilometre leg. The relay differs from the individual races in that there is a mass start, often the scene for some nasty pushing and shoving.

A discipline with very close links to cross-country is the **Nordic biathlon**, which consists of cross-country skiing and target rifle shooting. The skiers have to race round a circuit, stopping each time to shoot at a target. If a skier misses any of his shots, he must ski an extra distance on a short penalty circuit. However many shots he misses is the number of laps which he has to do on the penalty circuit. The rifles are carried on a shoulder strap at all times, and the shooting is made more difficult by the fact that they have to shoot from different positions each time (prone, standing, kneeling, etc.). A high standard of fitness will not only help the competitor to complete the cross-country sections more quickly, it will also help his marksmanship as his pulse rate will fall more quickly to a rate which is slow enough to allow his hands to remain steady. There is also an international team relay in biathlon.

Cross-country and biathlon require a level of cardiovascular fitness far higher than Alpine skiers', and more akin to that of distance runners. All the events are supreme endurance tests, and many of Britain's cross-country and biathlon teams are only able to stay in full-time training thanks to a co-operative employer: the Army. The applications of cross-country and biathlon in winter warfare are obvious. Britain's Nordic teams are also at an advantage in the skating events; because it is such a new technique, no teams have much experience of it and Britain can compete on level terms with the more established Nordic nations.

It must be said that cross-country skiing requires far less skill than Alpine skiing. For this reason, **Cross-country skiing requires less** people who are fairly fit can take **skill than Alpine skiing** it up relatively late in life (in the teens or twenties) and still get to a very high level through plain hard work. For the same reason, it is also an ideal participation sport for the older generation, who can wander through the woods on picturesque trails at their own pace, with no danger of falling and injuring themselves. The equipment is cheaper than for Alpine skiing, and many Alpine resorts, especially in Austria and Switzerland, now have plenty of well-marked trails through the woods.

The waxing of cross-country skis plays a very large role, but not quite for the same reason as in Alpine skiing. The object is to apply a *klister* of just the right stickiness to the area of the base directly beneath the foot, which stops the ski from sliding backwards as the skier pushes off from it. The rest of the base is then waxed with gliding wax, similar to Alpine wax, to make the ski run as fast as possible on the downhill sections and in the gliding phase between each push-off.

Cross-country skiers are able to do much of their basic conditioning training simply using endurance running to build up their stamina. Strictly speaking, cross-country races are not pure endurance events, because of the undulating terrain. The competitor has to work very powerfully on the uphill sections but can rest on the descents, and interval training is used to simulate this: a typical section would consist of 5 – 10 repetitions of a distance, anywhere between 100 metres and 1,000 metres, run at a fast pace with short breaks (2 or 3 minutes) in between to allow the heart rate to recover.

But running is not similar enough to cross-country skiing to be used exclusively. The pushing action of the arms must also be trained and there are now roller-skis which can be used, with specially sharpened sticks, on tarmac roads. The wheels contain a ratchet which prevents them from slipping back when the skier pushes off and the bindings can be adjusted to simulate skating or traditional technique.

The increased popularity of cross-country skiing amongst recreational skiers over the last decade, has prompted the ski manufacturers to produce skis which do not require the skilled waxing which is necessary for enjoyable cross-country skiing (there is nothing more frustrating than a ski which slips back every time you try to push forward off it, because it forces you to use the sticks to do all the pushing, soon causing aching arms, shoulders and back). The 'no wax' skis have an area of the base, beneath the boot where the *klister* would normally be applied, which has the texture of fish-scales. The scales are facing backwards, so that the sharp edges prevent the ski from slipping backwards but do not impede forward movement.

A similar invention, skins, have been in use for many years in the sport of **ski-touring** (trekking over high mountain terrain on skis). These are strips of sealskin which are attached to the skis, with the lie of the hairs facing backwards, thereby impeding backward movement but allowing forward movement. Quite steep slopes can be climbed using skins, something which is not possible with normal cross-country skis of either type.

Even competitive cross-country skiers have to resort, on the steeper climbs, to the **herringbone**, a method of climbing with the skis in a V, digging in the edges in a kind of backwards snowplough. It derives its name from the shape of the tracks left in the snow.

The skis used for ski-touring are more akin to Alpine skis than cross-country skis, and have proper edges, as quite long and steep descents are often made. Many people who go ski-touring now use special ski-touring bindings which will allow the heel to be raised during the ascents but will fasten it down during the descents. Ski-touring boots produced nowadays are also a hybrid, combining the support of Alpine boots with extra mobility and a good tread on the sole.

There is an old-fashioned technique for making turns with bindings which allow the heel to lift, called the **Telemark** technique after the region of Norway where it originated. The heel of the inside foot is lifted and the outside ski is thrust well in front of the inside ski, precisely the opposite to modern technique. Telemark has enjoyed a revival in recent years, especially in North America, and is now done, mainly on normal *pistes*, with skis which are as narrow as cross-country skis but with proper edges, and boots which are similar to ski-touring ones. There are even slalom competitions for Telemark skiers.

Ski-touring, on the other hand, derives its attraction from being an off-*piste* activity, where you can get away from the crowds and enjoy the solitude of the mountains. It is usually done in the spring months of April or May, when there is still plenty of snow but less chance of bad weather at the high altitudes which are reached. A typical ski-touring day will start at dawn (5 a.m.), when the group will set out from a high mountain hut and get the bulk of the ascending done before the snow gets too heavy. The descent to the next valley will probably be made in the early afternoon, when the spring snow is soft but not yet too slushy, and a long, leisurely meal will take place at the next overnight stop, followed by some sunbathing and an early night ready for the next early start. The mountain huts are spartan: some provide food, but you always have to carry your own bedding with you. The most popular ski-touring route is the Haute Route, from Chamonix to Zermatt, and it takes roughly a week. It is essential to go with a guide, who knows the terrain well and can judge the snow conditions correctly.

Ski-jumping, the other discipline of Nordic skiing, requires completely different physical qualities from cross-country: power, instead of stamina, and courage, instead of plain hard work. This is why the two sports were so dominant, during the winters, in their original home of Norway around the turn of the century. If you were not of the physical type to succeed at one of them, you would be very likely to be suited to the other. For the real all-rounders, there has always been the **Nordic combined**, a most unlikely combination of a highly technical explosive event and a relatively non-technical endurance event. It is as if the decathlon in track and field, were to be decided purely on the results of the pole vault and the 1,500 metres.

The shape of a Nordic ski-jump is very deceptive. At a glance, it would appear that the curved run-in would catapult the jumper upwards into the air, but a Nordic ski-jump is not like the kicker on a freestyle jump. The start of the run-in is very steep and gradually flattens out further down, but the take-off point is still on a downhill gradient. The landing area directly below the take-off point is also on a fairly flat gradient, but after a small distance it begins to get steeper. In order to generate enough upward momentum to clear the initial flat landing area, the ski-jumper must spring off the take-off area extremely powerfully, and at exactly the right moment.

Great heights and long distances are jumped, but as with the aerials in freestyle, the landing is safe

A ski-jumper in the first phase of his flight, soon after take-off.

because it is very steep and lessens the impact. In the area where the majority of the jumpers land, the gradient is at its steepest, and remains the same for roughly 40 metres. The middle of this area is known as the **Norm-point** of the jump. The size of the jump is usually defined by the distance from the take-off point to the Norm-point. For example, world-class competitions are always held on 70 metre and 90 metre jumps.

Further down the landing area from the Norm-point, at the end of the steep landing area, the gradient begins to flatten out gradually, at a point known as the **Critical point**. The reason for this name is clear: if the best jumpers begin to land too far beyond this point, they will be landing on a much flatter slope, with greater impact. So it is obvious that both the jumpers who fly greater distances than usual, and those who fly less, will be in danger, because they will be landing on a flat surface. The organizing committee take steps to ensure that most or all of the competitors land on the steepest part of the landing area. The lower-ranked jumpers go first with the best ones going last. If any of the first jumpers land beyond the Critical point, the competition is interrupted, the run-in is shortened (the jumpers go from a slightly lower point), and everyone has to start again. If any jumpers do not have enough power to get beyond the initial flat, the competition referee has the right to exclude them.

The results of the competition are decided on the total of the distance points and style points. The distance is measured, to the nearest half-metre, by judges lined up along the landing area. Any jumpers who are not able to reach the steep part of the landing area do not receive any distance points, as they have not come within the line-of-sight of the judges.

All jumpers are awarded style marks. The style judges look for a steady upper body while in mid-air, as little flapping of the skis as possible, and a clean landing, preferably in the Telemark position (one knee bent).

Strictly speaking, the physical quality needed by ski-jumpers is not pure power, but power-to-weight ratio. For this reason, the most successful jumpers tend to be thin but wiry. The fitness training which they do in the summer is based mainly around jumps and explosive strength.

Jumping technique can be worked on using plastic jumping hills. These are not made from Dendix, but from vertical strips of plastic, which are only suitable for skiing straight down the fall-line. The run-out area is covered with sawdust, which slows down the jumpers quickly and smoothly. These plastic hills are built on a large scale (up to 70 metre jumps) and there are even competitions held on them.

The technique of ski-jumping is more complex than simply exploding in an upwards direction off the take-off ramp at the right moment. To minimize the wind drag, the jumper must rotate forwards and stretch out his body in a horizontal direction, giving it the same aerodynamic properties as a wing, and enabling him to float a far greater distance. Because the skis are also horizontal, the best jumpers try to fly through the air in a slightly squint position, so that the body is not directly in the slipstream of the skis. This means that both the skis and the body will achieve the maximum wing effect.

There is one type of ski-jumping where the aerodynamic skills of the jumper are even more important, because the speeds involved are so much higher: **ski-flying**. This event is to standard 70 and 90 metre ski-jumping, what Downhill is to Slalom and Giant Slalom: far more dangerous, and more intimidating for even the most experienced jumpers. The world best in ski-flying is now approaching 200 metres, whereas for 90 metre jumps it is around 120 metres. These are only world bests, not world records, because every jumping hill is slightly different, and each one has a hill record, all of which now lie well beyond the Critical point for that hill. This causes problems, because the large crowds which often gather at World Cup ski-jumping events in Central Europe and Scandinavia demand a new hill record every time, and it is always unpopular when the judges decide to shorten the run-up (after unexpectedly long jumps by lesser-rated jumpers). The only way to provide longer world bests without forcing the jumpers to land on dangerously flat surfaces, is to build larger and larger ski-flying hills. This brings its own problems, as the take-off speeds become higher. Already they are over 80 mph, compared to 65 mph on 90 metre hills.

The equipment used in ski-jumping is more similar to cross-country than Alpine equipment. The boots are fairly soft but a little heavier than cross-country shoes and the bindings allow the heels to lift (necessary for the horizontal alignment of body and skis in mid-air). The skis are very long (roughly 240 centimetres) and very wide, with no edges and five grooves in the base, to keep the skis running straight on the run-up. The one-piece suits must be able to let through a certain amount of air, and are made to be baggy-fitting, as this helps the wing effect. Helmets are mandatory.

Most crashes in ski-jumping occur when the jumper is off-balance on landing and are not too serious. If the jumper crashes, or even puts a hand down, he loses most of his style marks and is effectively out of the competition. The worst crashes occur when the jumper gets wind from above on to the tips of the skis, flipping him over forwards. This can be his own fault from having rotated too far forward, or can be caused by an unlucky gust of wind. For this reason, jumping events are never held in high winds, something which caused the 1988 Olympic 90 metre jump to be postponed by a week. In doubtful conditions, the trainers will stand near the take-off point and only signal to their protégé to start their run-up when the air is calm.

Nordic Combined competitors have to deal with all these problems, on a 70 metre jump, in the first half of their event. They are then set off on a cross-country race at timed intervals which correspond to their performances in the jump. The winner of the jump sets off first and whoever gets to the finish first wins the overall event. The event is designed this way to make it easier for spectators to see the overall positions.

OTHER MEANS OF DESCENT

Two skis, one on each foot, are now no longer the only means of getting from the top to the bottom of the mountain. The **ski-bob**, a kind of bicycle with skis instead of wheels, has been in use for the last couple of decades in the Alpine countries.

The saddle has a well-sprung suspension beneath it to absorb the bumps. There is one short ski below the saddle area, and one further forward which is attached to the handlebars and can be pivoted to turn the bob. The rider wears short skis (roughly 30 centimetres long) on his feet, so that he can put them down for balance without braking.

There are World Cup and World Championship races for ski-bobs, which are held in all four Alpine disciplines. The Downhills are obviously not as demanding as those for ski-racers, with slightly smaller jumps and lower speeds. The Slaloms can be fairly dramatic: the slalom poles are hit by the handlebars of the bob, due to the strong inward lean which is necessary when tight turns are being made.

The **monoski** and the **snowboard** are more recent inventions than the ski-bob, but already they have overtaken it in popularity, probably because they

A monoskier in powder snow.

Agence Vandystadt/Jean Marc Barey

are less unwieldy and better suited to off-*piste* skiing.

The **monoski** is as long as a standard ski, but twice as wide so that two bindings can be mounted next to each other. The skier stands facing forward, with both legs clamped tightly together. This produces a technique which is extremely ungainly and inelegant.

The monoski forces the skier to make every turn on the outside edge of his inside foot, a position which is inherently unnatural and awkward. This is especially so on firm *pistes*. Monoskis are only really worth using in deep powder snow.

The monoski is still very popular in France, its country of origin, but it is quickly being superseded by the snowboard, especially in Austria and Germany. As its name suggests, the **snowboard** is designed to be used in a similar way to a surfboard or a skateboard. The stance, with the feet slightly parted and facing to the side, is very natural and conducive to good balance. Snowboarding is therefore easy to learn, and graceful and elegant to watch. It is quite feasible on firm, grippy *pistes*, but nearly impossible on icy ones. The snowboard comes into its own in powder, and like the monoski it will go faster than traditional skis in deep snow as it does not sink into the snow as much.

Snowboards can be fitted with conventional bindings, to be used with proper ski boots or with stiff plastic clamps which will hold your feet tightly even if you are wearing soft *après-ski* boots. No sticks are used, which makes it difficult for a snowboarder to propel himself along flat sections; normally he must remove one foot from the binding and push with it. The same method is used for travelling up draglifts.

There are now Slalom races for snowboarders, even on plastic slopes. Some resorts actually make the effort to build up giant banks of snow, similar in shape to the concrete skateboard parks of the 1970s.

Paragliding is not a sport that is necessarily connected directly with skiing as it is quite easy to

Tony Stone Worldwide/Mark Junak

get airborne by running down a very steep hill, but it has become popular in ski resorts because of the ease in getting up the mountain using the lifts, and the fact that it is easier to land while wearing skis as there is always some forward momentum. It is easy to learn, but once you have gained your confidence and are making long flights it is important to look out for sudden changes in weather, power cables and other vertical obstructions.

OFF-*PISTE* SKIING

'Going off-*piste*' is one of the great skiing experiences which all skiers fantasize about, and is often referred to as **powder skiing**. Unfortunately, the two things are not always the same: if you venture on to slopes which are not part of the prepared *pistes* of a resort, there is no guarantee that you will find snow which can be called powder. In fact, if you are planning to go off-*piste*, it is important to get to know the different types of snow conditions which can occur, both on and off the *pistes*. This understanding will still be useful if you have no fantasies about powder skiing and wish to remain a *piste*-basher for the rest of your life.

OFF-*PISTE* TECHNIQUE

When skiers are confronted with deep snow for the first time, most of them feel that they have to sit back to keep the tips on the surface of the snow. This is not necessary. It is, of course, also disastrous to lean forward in deep snow. If you stand in the middle of your skis, the curve of the tips will naturally prevent them from sinking in too deep. You only need to have the tips up at surface level for the initiation of the turn in order to be able to swivel the skis. This can be achieved with a well-defined up and down motion, causing weighting and unweighting of the skis. But, like all movements in deep snow, this must be done gently and not suddenly. It is also important to keep your weight distributed evenly on both skis, unlike on hard snow when you have to stand on the outside

Opposite:
A snowboarder wearing soft *après-ski* boots.

ski. In fact, if you look carefully, you will see that most falls in deep snow are caused by skiers leaning too far forward and standing too much on just one ski.

Since safety straps, which kept the ski attached to the leg even when the bindings had released, were replaced by ski-brakes, it has always been difficult to find a ski which has come off in deep powder. But this problem can now be solved using a new piece of equipment now available. It consists of a long thin strip of luminous material which you roll up and stuff up the leg of your ski trousers. One end is tied to your ski bindings, so that when your ski comes off the entire length of cord will be pulled out of your trouser leg and become unfurled. It can then guide you to your buried ski.

TYPES OF SNOW

All snow crystals begin their lives as snowflakes, falling gently from the sky. The first curious thing which you will notice about snowflakes when you spend some time in ski resorts, is that they are larger when the air temperature is relatively warm (e.g. just below 0°C), and much smaller when it is significantly colder. Indeed, when it is very cold, and the clouds begin to gather, the locals will often pessimistically state that they are not expecting much new snow, because it is 'too cold to snow'. They are usually right.

The weather forecasting in the Alps is more reliable than in Britain, because they **Weather forecasts in the Alps are** are not on the western edge of Europe **relatively reliable** like us and can plot the weather fronts accurately as they pass over France and Spain first. Poor Britain has to rely on weather ships and satellite pictures. So the Alps usually have warning of a big dump of snow, and they will even announce on the radio the altitude above which there will be snowfalls (below that it will fall as rain).

The temperature of the air at the time that the snow falls will dictate the moisture of the snow. If the air temperature is relatively warm (around 0°C), there will be much more water (in liquid form) contained in the snow, mixed with the solid snow crystals, than at, say, –10°C. The moisture in the snow tends to bind the crystals together, making the snow feel sticky. To check this, just use the snowball test: grab a handful of recently-fallen snow and squeeze it together. If the snow binds together into a solid snowball you are dealing with warm, wet snow. Cold, dry snow will fall apart. Ski resorts will pray for big dumps of wet snow early in the season, because it packs together so well to form a firm base which will keep the rocks covered. Once there is sufficient cover, most skiers will hope for falls of cold, dry snow, in other words, powder. Because of its light consistency, it is far easier to turn the skis in powder snow than in wet new snow, especially when there are several feet of the stuff.

Once the snow has stopped falling and the skies clear, the temperature will fall dramatically during the hours of darkness. The excess moisture in the snow will freeze, and the snow will become harder and firmer. The greater the moisture in the snow to start off with, the harder it will become overnight. But if the air temperature was already very low when the snow fell, the dry, powdery snow will not contain much moisture, and will not change dramatically during a clear night with low temperatures.

In the winter months of December and January, generally, a clear sunny day will not be warm enough to melt the snow sufficiently. But from February onwards, **spring snow** will form as the heat of the sun melts the tiny snow crystals and fuses them into larger grains, which is why this type of snow is also known as **granular snow**. As the temperature gets warmer, the spring snow becomes softer and wetter, until the end-product can only be described as slush. The Americans will sometimes refer to these conditions as sugary snow, but in Scotland it is simply called porridge!

Heavy, slushy snow can be very dangerous,

as it usually occurs at the end of the day when skiers are tired. Getting a ski caught under a pile of porridge can cause the slow, twisting type of fall which is awkward enough to break a leg but not always fast enough to cause the bindings to release.

When slush is exposed to a cloudless night, the sub-freezing temperatures will turn it into rock-hard ice. All you can do is pray that the resort had the foresight to run the *piste*-bashers over the runs the previous night, then you will at least have smooth ice to ski on. Woe betide you if the resort bosses forget to groom the *pistes* the day before when the snow is soft, but then try to correct their mistake the following morning when the snow is hard. The caterpillar tracks of the *piste*-bashers will undoubtedly make the snow smoother, but they will also break it up into thousands of little, hard lumps. To ski on these is like trying to ski on ball-bearings: difficult and unstable. These conditions are given many derogatory names, such as golf balls or frozen strawberries.

So wet slush will freeze hard during a clear night, and, conversely, dry, cold snow will remain soft and powdery. What happens to the snow when it is in between these two states: moist enough to form snowballs but not wet enough to have become granular? If groomed by *piste*-bashers, it will become ideal snow, firm but not actually icy, and very easy to grip and make turns on. But if left in its original state, the top layer will become firmer than what is beneath it, forming what is certainly the most difficult of snow conditions to ski on: **breakable crust**. The skis will sink into the snow, breaking through the hard crust, which will then hold the skis as if in a clamp and make it nearly impossible to initiate the turn by swivelling them. Last season, I tried to take a shortcut back to our hotel for lunch, after a morning of Downhill training, down a run which I thought had been groomed. At the best of times 223 centimetre skis are difficult to turn and when I discovered that I had ventured on to breakable crust I was reduced to doing jump turns, hopping a couple of feet into the air just to swivel the skis.

Breakable crust can also be formed from cold, dry powder at low temperatures, given the presence of one other ingredient, high winds. No matter how it is formed, breakable crust is best described by the derogatory term given to it by our American cousins, crud.

The ever-increasing use of **snow-cannons** to produce snow cover when temperatures are low but there is no snowfall, has led to a new type of snow, man-made. The first thing that struck me when I first encountered man-made snow in Bad Kleinkirchheim in 1980, was its consistency and regularity. Freshly produced man-made snow is the same all over the world, very firm, yet easy to grip. It is like ice but with a matt surface. The snow crystals in man-made snow are small and underdeveloped, because they do not have much time to form, as they drop from a height of roughly 50 metres having been propelled up there in the form of water droplets. Because the system only works at low temperatures, there is virtually no moisture in man-made snow. All in all, it is quite similar to the type of compact but dry snow which is produced naturally when powder snow is skied on and groomed at constantly low temperatures for several days. Of course, man-made snow can become granular when exposed to warm temperatures or sunshine, and when it freezes after that it will become icy and shiny. In fact, the first World Cup Downhill of the 1989/90 season, at Val Gardena, was held on man-made snow which was identical to naturally occurring frozen spring snow after it had been rained upon and then exposed to a cold, clear night. It was a reminder that slushy conditions can occur at any time of year, even in December, in this age of global warming.

When many prominent ski-racers, including Girardelli, Alberto Tomba and Peter Müller, were injured at the start of the 1989/90 season, a theory was put forward that man-made snow was dangerous as all these injuries had occurred upon it. This is certainly not the case. If anything, man-made snow is safer, because it is more compact and does not become rutted for racers with late start numbers. But the general shortage of snow meant that most race *pistes* were only covered with a few inches of (man-made) snow and none of the bumps and terrain of the ground underneath were levelled out, as is the case with a thick snow cover. Also, there was often only a thin strip of white, amongst brown fields, down which the race was held and any racer who crashed off the run (like Girardelli) would land on frozen earth instead of soft snow. In addition to these factors, the first Downhill was held at Val Gardena which is always a difficult course and especially so with a thin snow cover. Normally the Downhillers have a chance to regain their feel for speed at the start of the season on the easier Val d'Isère course, but in 1989/90 it had been cancelled. Opportunities for Downhill training had also been limited. So the fact that all the races were held on man-made snow was not in itself the reason for the large number of injuries.

MOGULS

Moguls are not exactly a snow type, but are a condition which occurs when a run is skied on by a large number of skiers over a long period of time (several days) without being groomed. As the first bumps begin to form, each skier begins his turn by swivelling his skis on the top of a bump and then finishing it in the trough below. This has the effect of digging out the trough even more, and piling more snow on to the bump below it.

The character of the bumps depends on the average length of ski of the skiers which form them. When the fashion for short skis was at its height, the bumps were very small and sharp and it was difficult for someone with longer skis to make turns through them. This is still the case in North America where the overall standard length is lower, but the moguls in Europe have become larger, with

Tony Stone Worldwide/Mark Shapiro

more space between them, over the last few years.

American resorts will usually groom most runs daily, but leave some others with bumps so that if you want to ski moguls you can. But in some Alpine resorts it is sometimes impossible to avoid moguls over a busy Christmas period.

Skiing moguls requires much practice, but apart from the above-mentioned technique of starting the turns on top of the bumps and finishing them in the troughs, the main principle is to be more active with the legs. They must act as shock absorbers, keeping the head as still as possible. For this reason, mogul skiing is very exhausting for the muscles of the legs and back.

Opposite: Moguls: note how the skier on the right is extending his legs into a trough, whilst the other two are bending their knees to absorb bumps.

HELI-SKIING

One of the problems facing keen off-*piste* skiers is that all ski resorts are becoming busier from year to year. This means that most of the slopes which are accessible using lifts will be extensively skied on within a few hours of a major snowfall. But the real pleasure of powder skiing is to carve your own track through deep, unblemished snow. **Heli-skiing** is the only way to guarantee these conditions. With most heli-skiing operations you also get the advantage of a qualified guide who will go with you to find the best powder and protect you from the risk of avalanches.

The main obstacle to a good heli-skiing trip is the weather. It needs to be fine and settled for the helicopter to be able to fly, and even with a local guide it is not safe to venture into remote terrain in poor visibility. But most heli-skiing operations are very aware of the effect which bad weather can have on a holiday, and they will usually offer a guaranteed minimum amount of vertical drop which you will ski during the week. If you lose a couple of days through bad weather at the beginning of the week, they will do their best to make up for it later on.

Heli-skiing is done in the Alps, but if you are going to invest in a heli-trip, which is not cheap at the best of times, I would recommend that you might as well go the whole hog and go to Canada, where the Rockies are far less overcrowded.

4 DIET AND FITNESS

DIET AND NUTRITION

I am often asked whether I adhere to any particular diet when I am competing and training in the Alps. My only answer is that it is impossible. During the racing period we are usually in a different country, eating a different style of food every week.

The only extra nutrition which I try to add regularly to the food we receive, are vitamin supplements. **Multivitamin tablets** are sufficient, along with extra **Vitamin C** tablets to ward off colds. This is especially useful for holidaymakers who are spending a week or two abroad, as the strains of germ and virus found in foreign countries are usually slightly different from those that the body's immune system is accustomed to. Fresh vegetables, a common source of Vitamin C, are often difficult to obtain in remote mountain villages.

When eating breakfast before a day's skiing, remember that the morning will be more energetic than usual if you have a desk job, so you will need to stock up on energy-supplying foods. This means eating plenty of **carbohydrates**, which are found in breakfast cereals and bread.

If you feel in need of a mid-morning snack, try to take a roll, or fruit, with you in a pocket, rather than a chocolate bar. Chocolate contains so much concentrated sugar, it can stimulate an insulin reaction in your body and actually lower your blood sugar level, making you feel less energetic.

Lunch at **mountain restaurants** will always be an expensive affair. They have the ultimate captive market and just to make sure of this, many restaurants will ban the consumption of packed lunches on their premises. If they are generous enough to set aside an area for consumption of packed lunches, it is very likely to be a draughty, unheated room in the basement. There is no simple solution, but if it is not too far down to the village, it is worth going down to find a reasonably-priced lunch. But beware the post-lunch queue on the lifts back up to the ski area. A good way of avoiding queues in general is to have an extremely early or late lunch, and get some skiing in while everyone else has gone for theirs.

The body becomes dehydrated more quickly at high altitude, because the air pressure is lower and water evaporates more easily. So make sure that you drink plenty of **water** before you set out for your day's skiing (drinking water is completely safe in all Alpine countries) and try to have **To avoid dehydration, drink plenty of** enough to drink with your lunch. **water before starting your day's skiing** Once again, the mountain restaurants charge exorbitant prices for drinks, but the only alternative is to take a flask with you in a rucksack or bumbag (a bag designed for skiers which fits around the waist). Alcoholic drinks will merely dehydrate your body even further.

Dinner is usually the main meal of the day on a skiing holiday, but it is advisable not to have it too early (e.g. immediately after finishing the day's skiing) as you will be hungry again before bedtime. Skiing, especially in cold weather, generates a large appetite and many tour operators' chalets offer tea and cakes in the afternoon, to take the edge off that appetite and to keep everyone going until dinnertime.

Conversely, it is best not to eat your evening meal too soon before retiring to bed, as your body must then expend energy to digest the food while you are sleeping, and it does not get as much chance to rest and regenerate itself.

Most people go on holiday, quite rightly, to relax and enjoy themselves, but it is easy to forget that alcohol has a stronger effect at high altitude.

I remember one incident at a British Ski Team training camp a few years ago at a high altitude summer ski resort, when we were given a break from training for a night and the following day. Due to the fact that none of us had touched alcohol for quite a while, combined with the effects of altitude, a couple of beers took a greater toll upon us than we expected. We then, unwisely, visited the local bowling alley, and ended up shot-putting the bowling balls through the air at the skittles! Needless to say, we were kicked out, and one of my team-mates was given a week's suspension by the team management. We all learnt our lesson the hard way, but every year young holidaymakers do the same and give the British a bad reputation in French and Austrian resorts. And it is no excuse to say that the Scandinavians are just as bad!

Evening drinking in the resort is a nuisance, but too many tipples in an *Alphütte* after lunch, before making the last descent of the day, is positively hazardous. This practice is far less common in France than in the German-speaking areas, where *Jägertee* and *Glühwein* are supposed to warm you up. This is a fallacy. Alcohol renders the body numb to the

Alcohol renders the body numb to cold but can accelerate the onset of hypothermia

cold, but if you drink it while still outside, it will accelerate the onset of hypothermia. The famous St Bernard rescue dogs carry not brandy but hot chocolate in the barrels around their necks nowadays, as a warm drink has been found to be more beneficial than an alcoholic one. I must admit, that if I were an intermediate skier sitting in an Alpine hut in the late afternoon, contemplating the last run of the day, when the snow is at its most slushy and most bumpy and when the visibility is at its worst, I would steer clear of the tipples and concentrate on avoiding collisions with the other skiers who had indulged!

FITNESS

The most difficult thing to do when trying to take up any new activity, physical or otherwise, is to get beyond the period when it is just a fad (i.e. the first two or three weeks), and to actually get into the habit of doing it. But if you want to get the most out of your skiing trip, you must exercise for two or three months before you go. One solution is to look at the sports which you are already in the habit of doing, and simply make an effort to do them regularly and energetically.

Racquet sports (squash, tennis and badminton) are all ideal ways of getting fit for skiing, because you not only have to do a lot of running, but also have to make sudden sideways changes of direction, when you are playing at a reasonable level. This prepares the legs for the explosive side-to-side movements of skiing turns.

Team games (football, rugby, hockey and basketball) are also good, because the swerves and side-steps used in these games also simulate turns on skis. But their major drawback is the risk of injury. If you do insist on playing football just before your skiing trip, the least you can do is make sure that you have insurance which will re-imburse you for the cost of your holiday if you sprain an ankle the day before your departure date.

Of the **endurance sports** (running, swimming and cycling) cycling is the most beneficial for skiers, because it develops leg strength. An exercise bike

Members of the British Ski Team mountainbiking during autumn training.

The Drambuie Liqueur Company

will do just as well, as long as you adjust the resistance so that you have to push fairly hard on the pedals and are not just coasting. Long-distance running does not really develop leg strength, and swimming even less so. But if you are an athlete competing in the sprint, long jump or triple jump events, this will definitely give your legs the explosive strength required for skiing.

If you happen to go ice-skating regularly, there could really be no better sport to prepare for skiing. If you are a good enough skater to take up figure skating or ice-hockey, this is even better, but once again, watch out for injuries.

It is still worth supplementing any of these sports with special exercise circuits geared towards skiing and, of course, if you are unable to do any of these activities, exercise circuits will be your only way of getting fit. These can be done at home, but if you already go to weight training or aerobics classes, just ask your instructor to give you extra exercises which will prepare you for skiing.

EXERCISE CIRCUIT

The following exercises will serve as a supplement to other activities, in which case you will need to do them at least once a week, or as a self-contained programme, where you would need to do them about three times a week.

Try to begin the exercise programme gently, working well within yourself, and only start to increase the intensity gradually after the first week. Always do a good warm-up, and always spend at least 15 minutes doing a warm-down after the exercise programme. This should consist mainly of stretching exercises, as muscles become shorter when they are exercised and need to be stretched afterwards so that they regain their original length. Stretching is important for the prevention of injury. If you prepare your body by getting it into unusual positions, it will be better equipped to handle the extreme positions which it will be forced into in a skiing fall.

There are leg, stomach, back and arm exercises in the following programme, and you should try to alternate between the different muscle groups. The legs are obviously the most important muscles for skiing, but the back is also frequently used, especially when skiing moguls. The stomach muscles also have to be well-conditioned in order to balance the back muscles and thereby avoid posture problems. The arms are less important, but still worth strengthening for the tasks of carrying skis, hanging on to draglifts and pushing along the flats.

WARM-UP

A gentle 10 minutes on the exercise bike or jogging is enough to get the heart and lungs going: your pulse rate should rise above 120 during the warm-up. You can check this if you have a watch with a second hand: simply find your pulse, in your wrist, neck, or by putting your hand over your heart, and count the beats for 10 seconds. Then multiply by six, to get the minute rate, which should be above 120. This can vary quite a bit, and if your normal, resting pulse is always very low (e.g. under 60), then your working pulse will also be lower.

EXERCISES
1 DOWNHILL POSITION

This is a similar exercise to the famous wall-sit, but better as it conditions the back and neck muscles as well as the legs. Just crouch down, with your knees at 90 degrees and your chest in a horizontal position over your thighs, feet slightly apart and elbows in front of the knees. Keep your head up, as if you had to look where you are going. This is the position that downhill skiers have to adopt for 2 or more minutes. You should begin by trying to hold it for 30 seconds, working up to 1 minute. Advanced skiers and racers should attempt to work up to 2 minutes.

2 KNEE BENDS

Stand with your feet slightly apart, bend down

until your knees are at 90 degrees and straighten again, keeping your back straight all the time. Start by doing 10, and work gradually up to 30 or 40. Very advanced skiers and racers can progress on to one-legged knee bends (also just down to 90 degrees), starting with 10 and working up to 30 or 40.

3 SIDE-TO-SIDE JUMPS

These are two-footed jumps, from side to side over a distance of about 1 metre. They should be done with a spring, so that you take off immediately after each landing. Start by doing about 20, and work up to 40. Advanced skiers and racers can progress on to GS jumps, jumping from outside leg to outside leg, or they can balance a broom handle on a couple of boxes and jump over that.

4 SIT-UPS

It is important not to do these with the feet jammed under wall-bars or furniture, as this only works the hip flexor muscles at the top of the thighs and not the stomach muscles proper. Start by lying on your back, with knees slightly bent and reach forward with straight arms to touch the knees. Start by doing

Martin Bell doing 'uphill situps'.

The Drambuie Liqueur Company

10 and work up to 20. Then you can begin to do sit-ups with your hands clasped behind your neck, touching your knees each time with the elbows. A further variation is twisted sit-ups, touching the left elbow to the right knee and vice versa. Advanced skiers and racers can progress on to sit-ups with the feet on a chair, also twisting to touch left elbow to right knee, etc.

With all these variations of sit-ups, it is important to curl and uncurl the spine, rather than just bending at the hips.

5 BACK-UPS

Lying on your stomach, raise your shoulders and legs simultaneously. Start by doing 10 and work up to 20. Advanced skiers and racers can use a table and lie face down on it, with the upper part of the body hanging over the edge. If you get a friend to hold your ankles down, you can then do dorsal raises, lifting and lowering your upper body. It will be more comfortable if you pad the edge of the table with a pillow.

6 PRESS-UPS

Start by doing around 10 and work up to 20 or 30. If you cannot manage conventional press-ups, you should begin with the so-called ladies' press-ups where the knees remain on the ground.

It is often overlooked that press-ups work the stomach muscles as well as the arms.

7 TRICEPS DIPS

From a seated position on a chair, stretch your legs out in front of you, grip the edges of the chair. Slide your feet forward until your behind is no longer on the chair and you are supported only by your feet and hands. Then bend and straighten the arms. Start with as many as you can easily manage and try to work up towards 20.

This arm exercise makes a change from press-ups, and is very useful in preparing the arms for the pushing action with ski sticks.

You should not aim your sights too high at first, in terms of the number of repetitions of each exercise, but you should always try to do the whole circuit through three times. Afterwards, you should do the following stretching exercises as a warm-down, with perhaps another 5 minutes' gentle jogging or exercise biking thrown in.

STRETCHING EXERCISES
1 HEAD CIRCLING

Graham Bell performs an advanced stretching exercise for the hip joints.

Keeping the shoulders still and level, circle the head through 360 degrees, 10 times in each direction, in a slow and relaxed manner. Stretches the muscles of the neck.

The Drambuie Liqueur Company

2 ARM CIRCLING

With straight arms, circle them backwards 10 times and forwards 10 times in circles as wide as possible and at a fairly brisk pace. Stretches and mobilizes the shoulders.

3 HIP CIRCLING

Keeping head and feet still and with hands on the hips, circle the hips through wide circles, ten in each direction. Mobilizes the hips, to help angulation when skiing.

The following exercises must be done slowly, gradually increasing the stretch, without bouncing, for about 30 seconds. It must not feel painful, merely tight.

4 SPLITS

You do not need to be able to do the complete splits, just stand with your legs straight and as far apart as possible. Then bend one knee to stretch the inside of the leg which is straight. Hold for 30 seconds, then do the same on the other leg.

5 HAMSTRING STRETCH

Place one straight leg on a table and gradually try to bend your head towards your knee, holding it for 30 seconds, then do the same for the other leg.

6 HIP FLEXOR STRETCH

Start by kneeling on the ground, then place one foot (e.g. the left one) on the ground in front of you so that the left knee is at right angles. Then push your hips forward so that the muscles on the front of the right thigh become tight. It will be easier if you have a table or high-backed chair in front of you to hold on to. If you find it too easy, grab your right foot with your right hand and pull it up to your behind before pushing the hips forward. Hold the position for 30 seconds for each leg.

7 THIGH STRETCH

Place one foot on a chair and bend that knee until your behind approaches your heel. This should stretch the front of the thigh. If not, try standing on one leg and pulling the other foot up behind you, leaning forward slightly with the upper body. Hold for 30 seconds with each leg.

8 CALF MUSCLE STRETCH

Standing on the edge of a step, let your heels hang down over the edge, stretching the calf muscles, hold for 30 seconds. Try to do the exercise with both a straight knee and with a bent knee, as these different positions stretch different muscles in the calf. If you cannot stretch the muscles sufficiently standing on both feet, try standing on one foot at a time, to put more pressure on the calf.

The same position can be used to do a calf-strengthening exercise, rising up and down on the toes.

9 FOOT CIRCLING

Raise one foot in the air, and circle it through wide circles, 10 times in each direction. Then repeat with the other foot. Skiers' ankles can become weak and stiff through the exaggerated support of plastic boots. This exercise and the preceding one, can rectify that.

Once you are actually on your skiing trip, it is advisable to go through this stretching routine each morning in your room, to warm up for your day's skiing and to protect yourself from injury.

ADVANCED FITNESS TRAINING

As a full-time ski-racer, I do at least two fitness training sessions a day, during the periods when I am back home in Britain. Throughout the build-up period from June until November, this takes up around three hours of my time each day. Over these months, a two-week training camp in the Alps will be followed by a two-week period at home. While abroad, four or five hours each morning are spent skiing on the glacier, and one or two hours each afternoon are devoted to fitness training. This conditioning is geared more towards maintaining fitness rather than increasing it, so that the racer's strength is saved for the next day's skiing.

The bulk of the hard work is done back in Britain and includes running, cycling and swimming for endurance, interval sprints over distances ranging from 200 metres to 600 metres, short explosive sprints over 30 – 100 metres, bounding and hopping routines for explosive strength, weight training for legs, arms, stomach and back, and of course regular stretching routines. All this hard work is interspersed with as many different games and activities as possible, to make training more fun and to improve co-ordination and balance.

TRAINING ON SKIS

The best fitness training for skiing is skiing itself. Long runs without stopping will build up leg strength in all the right muscles. If there are no long runs available (e.g. on the glacier) an ideal substitute is to make the occasional run on one ski. It does not require a run of much length to soon build up leg strength in this way.

It would be ideal to compensate for the shortness of dry ski slopes in Britain by the occasional run on one ski, but the overall difficulty of holding an edge on plastic makes it technically difficult. It is, however, possible for young racers to build up fitness on dry slopes by doing very short turns, known as **shortswings**.

Grass skiing is a better way for young racers to improve their fitness than dry slope racing, as the runs are longer and all aspiring racers should try to do both during the summer.

Whatever activities you do to get fit for skiing, try to enjoy them in the knowledge that your own skiing will become more enjoyable as your standard improves through increased fitness.

5 LEARNING FROM OTHERS

The drawback of most weekend sports TV programmes is that they are generally watched by sports enthusiasts who are themselves participating in their favourite sports at the weekends. *Ski Sunday* is no exception in this respect: many of its potential viewers spend their weekends skiing in Scotland or on dry slopes, but fortunately the advent of the video recorder has resolved this problem to a great extent. When you do get the chance to watch top-level skiing on television, you can always improve your own standard by watching the racers and trying to visualize yourself going through the same motions, no matter whether you are an aspiring racer or just ski for fun.

Watching top-level skiing on TV can help you to learn and improve

SLALOM

When watching Slaloms on television, it is easy for the eye to be distracted by the slalom poles, which are battered in every direction by the racers as they go past. But it is more important to watch the racers' feet, knees and hips, and to try to see what effect this has on the behaviour of their skis.

The turns which have to be made in Slalom are of a very short radius and the construction of the skis makes it impossible to carve these turns completely. So the skis have to be swivelled on the snow at the beginning of the turn, until they are almost pointing towards the next gate. This can only be done if there is virtually no weight on the skis (this is the **upweighting** phase of the turn) and often the racer is actually a couple of inches off the ground at this point. When he lands, or at least puts pressure on his skis once more (the **downweighting** phase of the turn), the skis will be on edge. If the racer's

Pirmin Zurbriggen, the supreme all-rounder, in Slalom.

Bob Thomas Sports Photography/Johnson

body position is good (well-angulated knees and hips) and if his edges are sharp enough, the ski will grip immediately as soon as pressure and weight are applied to it. If you can clearly see that a racer's body is fairly straight and upright, it can mean that he will find himself skidding on the steeper turns, although it is possible to use much less angulation on the flatter and straighter sections of a course. Norway's new Slalom star, Ole-Christian Furuseth, clearly demonstrates knee angulation in a dramatic way, with his long, skinny legs. He appears to be permanently out of control because of his bandy legs, but if you watch his outside leg in each turn you can see that the knee is extremely bent and angled into the slope, guaranteeing good edging and grip. Furuseth's individual style means that his upper body is often bent quite far forward to compensate for his hips, which are usually fairly far back, as if he was sitting in a chair. This ensures that his centre of gravity is always over the middle of his ski (not too far forward or back), and coupled with his obvious aggression this makes him both fast and reliable. He is no flawless technician and other racers often say that he skis as if he has a basketball gripped between his knees.

The importance of standing in the middle of the skis has been mentioned and on the slow motion replays which are shown when a Slalom racer blows out of the course, you will usually see him sitting back and in trouble for a couple of gates before falling or blowing out, a sure sign that disaster is on its way. The trouble is, that all racers have to get back on to the tails of their skis slightly at the end of the turn to gain acceleration. It is only when they overdo it and cannot get their centre of gravity forward for the next turn that they lose control. The Italian, Alberto Tomba, double Olympic Champion of 1988, is notable for being always very much over the middle of his skis. His superb timing means that he can dispense with exaggerated up and down weighting and excessive sitting back at the end of the turn, in both Slalom and Giant Slalom. This has the effect of making him look static, normally a fault, but his smoothness and lack of skidding ensure that he is fast, although he does not appear so. He is always in a relatively upright position, which saves energy and leg strength. He is said to be less fit than he should be, but this does not matter so much because he has developed an economical style of skiing to make up for it. Ingemar Stenmark, possibly the best Slalom skier ever, had a similar style and was very impressed with Tomba at the 1988 Olympics. Recently, Tomba has been less dominant, however, and who is to say that he would not be even more consistent if he paid more attention to his fitness training.

When it comes to pure strength, Marc Girardelli, the Austrian who has raced for Luxembourg ever since his father had a dispute with the Austrian Ski Federation, is probably the most powerful Slalom racer on the circuit, and this has enabled him to take up Downhill fairly late in his career with great success. In fact, in the 1989 season he became the first-ever skier to win World Cup races in all four disciplines. In Slalom, he was one of the last racers to bring both hands around the right side of the pole, and only recently has he begun to wear a slalom helmet and take the poles across the body. He was able to retain the traditional style for so long because he always takes a very early line through the course. This means that whenever he approaches a pole, he has already completed his turn and his skis are pointing in the direction of the next gate. This is also known as skiing a round line, or skiing from behind. The opposite happens when a racer gets late and in the slow motion replays you will often see a racer getting later and later, turning after the pole instead of before it, until he skids past a gate, unable to get round it. This almost always happens on steep sections: on the flats you can afford to get late and get away with it.

Another facet of Slalom technique which Girardelli demonstrates clearly, is the use of the **scissor step**. As he finishes his turn, his outside

Opposite:
Pirmin Zurbriggen
in Downhill.

ski is not always pointing towards the next gate, but he can step on to his inside one, which is. As he does this, he upweights and his inside ski becomes the outside ski for the next turn. The scissor step reduces the amount of turning that the outside ski needs to do, as part of the change in direction is achieved by the step, and less turning means more speed. If you watch a Slalom race on a dry ski slope, you will see that the turns of the top racers consist almost entirely of scissor steps, as it is nearly impossible to carve turns on plastic because no platform of snow is built up below the ski to hold it in the turn, as is the case on snow.

Another useful point for young racers to watch out for on TV is the way that top Slalom racers ski through a *verticale* (a set of gates straight down the fall-line). They turn no more than is necessary going almost straight and gaining a lot of speed. The problems come when they reach a very tight turn after the *verticale* carrying a lot of speed.

DOWNHILL

One of the most successful Downhillers of the past few years has been a Swiss racer who became European Junior Downhill Champion in 1980, but then concentrated on Giant Slalom and made his initial breakthrough on the World Cup circuit in that discipline. He did not win his first Downhill until 1985, but he chose the toughest course in the world to do it on, at Kitzbühel, winning two races in two days there and a further one on the same course in 1987. Pirmin Zurbriggen is not stylish to watch, with his arms held high and straight and used freely to maintain balance, though not as wildly as the arms of Franz Klammer, the now-retired Austrian who was the most successful Downhiller in the history of the World Cup. Like with Klammer, you have to watch Zurbriggen's legs to see why he is so fast and they are always doing the right things. His knee angulation is clearly visible on the tighter and icier turns of the Downhill courses, and he is master at getting on to the tails of his skis at the

end of the turn, something which is as important in Downhill as in Slalom for gaining acceleration. In fact, he sits back so much that it has been known to cause him to crash on at least one occasion. His tuck is aerodynamically good, and his one minor weakness is jumping. He is normally compact in the air off jumps and does not lose time, but he has crashed a couple of times on them. He has been lucky never to have had a major injury which has kept him out for more than a few weeks.

Peter Müller, another Swiss, has won more Downhills than anyone except Klammer. When he first started winning, back in the late 1970s, he was scornfully described as being a glider, someone who could only do well on flat, easy courses. But although he has never won Kitzbühel, he has long since proved that he can turn, not least by winning a couple of Super G races. **Gliding**, that ability to go fast in a straight line on the flatter sections of the course, consists of several factors. You have to be big and heavy, and you need a fast pair of skis with a base well suited to the snow temperature and humidity on the day; a skilled ski technician to prepare the skis with the correct wax; a good, low, aerodynamic tuck, and to be standing on a flat ski, something which is not as easy as it sounds, as many people stand permanently on their outside edges slightly, or more commonly on their inside edges slightly, especially when it is bumpy and slick. You also need to be soft over the little bumps, and it is said that you can tell a good glider because his skis make less noise than other racers as they slap over an uneven section. Müller has all these qualities. His tuck sometimes appears to be too much of a sitting back position, but this allows him to absorb the small bumps more softly. Müller has always had a slight weakness over jumps, with two notable crashes in 1986, one at Are, Sweden, and one on the last jump of the last race of the season at Whistler, Canada, where he was half a second ahead of everyone else and would have won the Downhill title if he had stayed on

The Drambuie Liqueur Company

his feet. And as I write this, Müller is out of action with a broken knee after crashing on the notorious Camel Bumps at Val Gardena. He is past the usual retirement age for ski racers and who knows if we will see him back again for the 1990/91 season.

Another victim of the Camel Bumps in 1989 was Michael Mair, the Italian who, at over 100 kilos, is the largest racer on the circuit. For this reason he is always fast on the straight sections of a course, although he can turn as well. It is a fact you must bear in mind when watching ski-racing that big racers always look untidy and not particularly fast, even if they are skiing well. On the other hand, small racers always look fast and aggressive, even if they are going slowly, because their body

Ronald Duncan, of Britain, gliding in a low, aerodynamic tuck position.

movements are always quicker.

The Canadians have been a familiar sight in their bright yellow suits ever since Read and Podborski started winning in the late 1970s. The current number one Canadian, Rob Boyd, has already won three World Cup races and is an excellent demonstrator of the art of **squashing** or **pressing** jumps in Downhill. This is done by pushing the hands and the whole upper body forward and down at the moment of take-off. This stops the airflow from getting under the ski tips and flipping the racer backwards, the most common cause of crashing on jumps. It also gets the racer back down to the ground as quickly as possible, as time spent in the air is time wasted.

Compressions are another problem which Downhillers have to deal with. Watching them can teach you how to handle similar terrain when you are freeskiing. A compression is where a steep section is followed suddenly by a flat, or even uphill, section. Strong legs are needed to resist the downward force and it is vital to stay forward. You will see plenty of crashes in compressions like the rollercoaster at the finish at Kitzbühel, caused by racers sitting back.

GS AND SUPER G

In some ways, these disciplines are more difficult than Slaloms and Downhills. They are more exhausting because they are longer than Slaloms and the body is more active than in a Downhill, as there are more turns. They are technically harder too. In Downhill the whole turn can be carved; in Slalom none of the turn is carved, you are merely jumping from side to side.

But in GS and Super G, the first half of the turn is done by swivelling the ski and the second half is carved. The sooner in the turn you can get the ski carving cleanly, the quicker you will be. On the straighter and flatter sections of courses, it is possible to carve the whole turn.

Lars-Boerje Eriksson, from Sweden, is of slight build and his Swedish nickname, Bulan, loosely translates as Stumpy. But he almost always carves his turns cleanly, and this has helped him to win World Cup GSs and Super Gs.

Martin Bell getting on to a poma lift.

6 SKI SAFETY

PISTE ETIQUETTE

Ski resorts are becoming ever more crowded, especially when snow is scarce, so it is more important than ever to obey the following rules, both for your own safety and that of other skiers.

1. Give priority to slower skiers ahead of you when overtaking them. It is up to the faster skier to avoid the slower skier and the faster skier is to blame if there is a collision.
2. Never ski faster than your ability. You should be in control at all times, and if the terrain or visibility is difficult you should reduce your speed accordingly.
3. Never stop on a *piste* in any of the following places: below a blind rise, in a narrow section or just around a bend.
4. If you fall, on the *piste* or the draglift, move out of the way as quickly as possible. Do not hold on to the draglift bar if you have fallen and are being dragged up on your stomach.
5. When setting off or joining a new *piste*, look carefully uphill and downhill and give way to other skiers who are already skiing on that *piste*.
6. Never walk in the middle of the *piste* (e.g. if you have lost or broken a ski). Keep to the edge.
7. Obey all signs and markers, especially when runs are marked as closed due to avalanche danger.
8. Never ski off-*piste* alone.
9. If you see an accident, you must stop and ask if the skier is OK. If you are involved in a

collision, you must give your name and address. If a skier is injured, plant a pair of skis in the snow in a crossed position to warn others. Keep the injured skier warm and do not move him or her unless it is absolutely necessary. Send someone, preferably a good skier, to get help from the ski patrol, first making sure that they know the exact position of the accident. Someone must always stay with the injured skier.

10. The most efficient way to carry your skis is on the shoulder, tips pointing forwards. However, when walking through crowded areas, take great care that the tails of your skis do not swing round and hit someone on the head.

AVALANCHES

As a Downhill racer, I can assure you that far more skiers lose their lives while skiing off-*piste* than while racing. By far the two most common fatal situations are skiing over a precipice and being caught in an avalanche.

It would seem obvious that you are far more likely to ski over a cliff in bad visibility, but of course you should never ski over a blind rise at any time if you do not know what is **Never ski over a blind rise without** on the other side. In bad weather you **knowing what's on the other side** should only venture off-*piste* if you, or a companion (ideally a qualified guide), know the terrain off-by-heart. Even if the weather appears fine and there are only a few wispy patches of fog wafting around, remember that it will be very disorientating once you are inside one of these patches.

Another advantage of a local guide is that he will know which slopes are the most likely to suffer avalanches, but you also use your own knowledge to avoid them. Avalanches are always likely after a large fall of new snow and especially so when that snow has fallen on to a base of smooth ice upon which it will slide easily. Large areas of breakable crust on steep slopes will often form slab avalanches, where large areas of crust break away and slide, with the dry powder beneath acting as ball-bearings.

Warm weather with a thaw is another dangerous time for avalanches, as the snow becomes wetter and therefore heavier, until it can no longer support its own weight. This is especially common on the grazing pastures at lower altitudes, where the snow will slide easily over the wet grass, and on south-facing slopes where the snow will quickly become wet and heavy.

If, God forbid, you should find an avalanche bearing down upon you, you must decide whether you can out-ski it, depending on the size and distance of the avalanche and your own ability and confidence. If you cannot, it is generally accepted that it is safer to remove your skis and sticks, so that they will not tangle you up. Once inside the avalanche, you are supposed to make swimming movements to try to keep yourself as near the surface as possible. As soon as you feel yourself coming to a halt, try to form a snow-free space in front of your face with your arms, which will give you some air to breathe. Then, if you are well and truly buried, all you can do is wait and hope that you will be dug out. There is no point in wasting your breath shouting for help, as the snow will deaden all noise.

If you are a keen off-*piste* skier, I would recommend that you fit the Recco radar reflectors on to the back of your boots. If the resort has helicopters fitted with the detection equipment, and conditions are good enough for them to fly in, you will be found. This assumes that someone has reported you as missing, and you should therefore never ski off-*piste* alone and should inform someone on-*piste* of your intention. If you are the one to survive, try to mark the point where your companions were last seen. Only go to alert the rescue services if they are nearby, otherwise it is better to begin the search yourself as time is of the essence.

FROSTBITE

Frostbite is not just a hazard of off-*piste* skiing, but it is more likely to occur when you are making a long descent rather than on a short run. It is most easily detectable on the face, where your companions will immediately warn you of a deathly white patch. It is imperative to place a warm hand on the affected area at once, and to get indoors as quickly as possible.

Frostbite of the feet is far more dangerous, as it cannot be readily seen. As a rule of thumb, once you have lost all feeling in your feet it is only a matter of time before they become frostbitten, if the temperature is low enough. You should never ski for too long with numb feet without at least checking them indoors every now and then.

People who have suffered frostbite once will be more vulnerable to the cold in future, and of course the worst cases can necessitate the amputation of all five toes. So frostbite is definitely something for you to be on your guard against.

7 USEFUL INFORMATION

ADDRESSES

The Home Nations governing bodies can give you the dates of races in those countries on dry ski slopes and, in the case of Scotland, on snow.

British Association of Ski Instructors
Inverdruie Visitors Centre
Inverdruie
Aviemore
Inverness-shire
PH22 1QH

British Dry Ski Slope Operators Association
Ski Rossendale
Haslingden Old Road
Rawtenstall
Rossendale
Lancashire
BB4 8RR
(0706) 228844

British National Grass Ski Congress
Brocades House
Pyrford Road
West Byfleet
Surrey
KT14 6RA
(0932) 336488

British Ski Federation
Brocades House
Pyrford Road
West Byfleet
Surrey
KT14 6RA
(0932) 336488

English Ski Council
Area Library Building
The Precinct
Halesowen
West Midlands
B63 4AJ
(021) 501 2314

Ski Club of Great Britain
118 Eaton Square
London
SW1W 9AF
(071) 245 1033

Ski Council of Wales
PO Box 3
Chepstow
Gwent
NP6 6NJ

Scottish National Ski Council
110a Maxwell Avenue
Bearsden
Glasgow
G64 4BR
(041) 943 0760

Ulster Ski Council
43 Ballymaconnell Road
Bangor
County Down
Northern Ireland
(0247) 473134

Austrian National Tourist Office
30 St George Street
London
W1R 0AL
(071) 629 0461

French Tourist Office
178 Piccadilly
London
W1V 0AL
(071) 499 6911

Italian State Tourist Office
1 Princes Street
London
W1R 8AY
(071) 408 1254

Spanish Tourist Office
57-58 St James's Street
London
SW1A 1LV
(071) 499 0901

Swiss National Tourist Office
Swiss Centre
New Coventry Street
London
W1V 8EE
(071) 734 1921

BOOKS AND MAGAZINES

BOOKS:
The British Ski Federation's Guide to Better Skiing by John Samuel (Pan Books 1986)
Skiing Real Snow by Martyn Hurn (Crowood 1987)

MONTHLY MAGAZINES:
Ski Survey (the official magazine of the Ski Club of Great Britain)
The Skier
Skiing UK
Ski Magazine
Daily Mail Ski
The Good Skiing Guide

DATES AND VENUES

Jan/Feb 1991, Saalbach, Austria, World Championships
Feb 1992, Albertville, France, Winter Olympic Games
Feb 1993, Japan, World Championships
Feb 1994, Lillehammer, Norway, Winter Olympic Games

8 GLOSSARY

abfahrt downhill ski run
aerials freestyle discipline involving jumps
alm mountain pasture
anti-friction pad slippery pad behind toepiece of binding
babylift wire held at waist height, sometimes with bar, used on nursery slopes
ballet freestyle discipline
base underside (part which runs on snow) of ski
BASI British Association of Ski Instructors
basket disc near base of ski pole
bib fabric showing competitor's number
binding device screwed to ski into which ski boots fasten
bloodwagon sledge to transport injured skiers
brake springloaded prongs to stop runaway skis
breakable crust hard-surface snow, soft underneath
British Development Squad run by British Ski Federation for the best British ski-racers aged between seventeen and twenty-one
British Seed Points ranking system used for ski-racing in the UK
bubble gondola lift
bum-bag small pack attached to belt
button-lift one-person draglift with disc instead of bar
cable-car access lift to snow area
camber arched shape of ski when no weight is applied
carved turn turn in which ski moves in its own track without skidding

chairlifts two–four person open lifts on which the skier is seated

compression terrain where ground flattens or rises

cornice overhang of snow at top of slope caused by wind

couloir steep, narrow descent between cliffs

crevasse crack in glacier ice, often covered by snow

cross-country travelling over flat terrain using thin skis and lightweight shoes

Dendix plastic bristles used for dry ski slopes

Derbyflex metal plate with layer of rubber fitted between ski and binding to allow for slightly greater flexibility of ski

detachable quads chairlifts which detach from wire at top and bottom, also known in USA as line-munchers because of their high capacity

DIN German standards organization for equipment design

downweighting when the skier lands on or puts pressure on his skis

draglift system of cables by which skiers are pulled up the slopes

edges border round base of ski to help it grip

FIS *Fédération Internationale de Ski*, the world governing body of skiing

FIS points international ranking system for ski-racing

föhn warm wind creating thaw

forerunners skiers who ski down a course just before a race begins

funicular steep cable railway

glacier skiing skiing on snow retained all year by the cooling effect of a mass of ice beneath it

gliding ability to go fast in a straight line on the flatter sections of a course

glühwein hot, mulled wine

gondola cabin cableway for two–six persons also known as *télécabine* or bubble

granular snow *see* spring snow

grass skiing skiing with short caterpillar-tread skis on grassy slopes

groove divides the base of the ski down the middle to help keep ski straight when not turning

herringbone backwards snowplough used to climb a slope

hot-dogging pastime from which freestyle developed

Jännerloch January hole – quiet two weeks for resorts after Christmas holiday period

klister special sticky wax used on cross-country skis

langlauf cross-country skiing

line-munchers *see* detachable quads

moguls bumps formed by skiers on a *piste*

monoski single ski as long as standard ski but twice as wide into which both boots fit side by side

motorway broad, easy *piste*

mountain guides the only people qualified to take clients off-*piste*

Nordic biathlon competition combining cross-country and target rifle shooting

Nordic combined combination of cross-country and ski-jumping

nursery slopes gentle slopes where beginners can learn to ski

off-*piste* skiing away from prepared and patrolled runs

piste prepared and patrolled run, usually with firmer snow

poma type of button-lift

porridge wet, heavy snow

powder new, light-textured snow

ratrac vehicle for preparing *pistes* (aka: snowcat, *piste*-basher)

reverse camber shape of ski when weighted

Schuss straight run down a slope

shortswings very short turns

sidecut hourglass shape of ski

side-slip controlled sideways slide

sidestepping upwards climbing technique

ski-bob like a bicycle with skis instead of wheels

ski guide provided by tour operator to offer advice

Agence Vandystadt/Didier Givois

and information about resort

ski-touring trekking over high mountain terrain on skis

ski-stopper *see* brake

snowboard boards designed to be used in a similar way to a surfboard or skateboard

snow-cannon spray water under pressure from nozzles positioned on main runs to form snow

snow cement spreading of coarse salt/fertilizer on slushy snow to produce hard surface, now rarely used as it shrinks glaciers and causes pollution

snowseed competitor used as forerunner, also known as powder seed or snowplough

spring snow large snow grains caused by tiny snow crystals melting in the sun and fusing together, also known as granular snow

Marc Girardelli in a Super G.

steilhang (German) steep slope

stem outward fanning of skis into slight snow-plough

straddle in Slalom when the tip of the inside ski goes just on the wrong side of the pole

tail back end of ski

T-bar two-person draglift with T-shaped bar attached to an overhead wire

Telemark method of turning using cross-country bindings

tip front end of ski

traverse skiing across a slope

tuck low aerodynamic crouch used by Downhillers

upweighting when a skier puts virtually no weight on the ski

wedge fits between ski and binding to compensate for bow-legs or knock-knees

white-out poor visibility weather conditions